Enneagram

A Complete Guide to the Search for Harmony

(Complete Guide to Test and Understand Personality Types)

Nicolas Contreras

Published By **John Kembrey**

Nicolas Contreras

Enneagram: A Complete Guide to the Search for Harmony (Complete Guide to Test and Understand Personality Types)

ISBN 978-1-998038-71-8

No part of this guidebook shall be reproduced in any form without permission in writing from the publisher except in the case of brief quotations embodied in critical articles or reviews.

Legal & Disclaimer

The information contained in this book is not designed to replace or take the place of any form of medicine or professional medical advice. The information in this book has been provided for educational & entertainment purposes only.

The information contained in this book has been compiled from sources deemed reliable, and it is accurate to the best of the Author's knowledge; however, the Author cannot guarantee its accuracy and validity and cannot be held liable for any errors or omissions. Changes are periodically made to this book. You must consult your doctor or get professional medical advice before using any of the suggested remedies, techniques, or information in this book.

Table Of Contents

Chapter 1: The Perfectionist

The Perfectionist is a person on a venture who desires to enhance themselves and the arena round them in some component manner they will have the capacity to steer it. They are unflagging of their efforts to conquer every challenge and are specially driven to defeat any obstacle that is perceived thru them to be ethical in nature. They do that with a preference to assist free the excellent part of themselves and allow it to contribute to the human enjoy. The Perfectionist in no manner stops striving for the first-class feasible values, although it approach they should sacrifice a terrific deal of their very own with a purpose to do so.

Looking via our facts, we can see that Perfectionists are frequently the ones specific individuals who artwork toughest to make a difference and to reply a better calling. Extraordinary figures like Gandhi and Joan of Arc are belief to be Perfectionists due to their willingness to sacrifice an smooth life inside the try to perform a little thing that might honestly be counted.

A Perfectionist may additionally have immoderate ideals, however they are moreover some of the most sensible of humans. Their goal is to be of provider to humanity due to the truth they may be dedicated to the perception that they may be on a challenge. This might be a exceptional-human project just like the heroes stated above, however it moreover could be a small, mundane and absolutely project like making their environment slightly greater orderly.

Perfectionists do have a sturdy, well-advanced sense of task, however further they normally feel that it's miles critical for them to defend their actions to others round them—but even to themselves, at times. The gain of this manner of thinking is that Perfectionists are very thoughtful approximately all functionality effects that could stem from their actions. They are very controlled, and frequently reflect for a bargain of time to make certain that they themselves take a look at their excessive, inflexible inner requirements. Thanks to this addiction, Perfectionists usually view themselves as cerebral and rational, who're ruled thru a dedication to first-rate judgment, objectivity, and truth. However, this is not honestly the case. In fact, another way of searching on the Perfectionist is as an activist or a reformer who is searching out a socially best purpose for what they experience they want to do. Far from emotionally vain, the Perfectionist is glaringly someone of passion and intuition. He or she has a bent to apply instinctive convictions and judgments at the manner to manage and direct their movements—and the behavior of others.

In creating a regular, concerted try and stay actual to their thoughts, Perfectionists attempt to keep away from being caused with the resource in their instincts and passions, actively resisting them or repressing them as an entire lot as possible. Because of this constant attempt, what emerges is a individual kind that has struggles with resistance, repression, and— even at times aggression. Other human beings commonly perceive Perfectionists as very self-managed, to the element of seeming inflexible. However, Perfectionists undergo due to this misperception as they have got a unique internal enjoy. For them, it appears as though they're struggling to maintain a decent lid on a cauldron that threatens to bubble over with passions and goals. The attempt to hold everything down is often large, and that they face extreme worry that they may in the end explode—to the detriment of all and sundry spherical them. This is the primary deliver of suffering confronted with the resource of a Perfectionist.

As the decision can also suggest, the Perfectionist believes that being uncompromisingly strict with themselves, they will in the long run be able to emerge as "best." This will cause them to experience actually really worth of themselves—and they hope it's going to cause them to revel in cherished through others. However, this attempt to create their personal concept of what perfection is always leads them to be trapped in a non-public hell of their very very own format. From this entrapment, they have got hassle understanding the manner to agree with their inner steering tool. Nor can they consider lifestyles itself. This way that Perfectionists often talk over with their kids mastering (additionally called the superego) due to the fact they agree with that this voice may be able to help to manual them in the path of what they attempting to find so passionately: the greater suitable. While it's far feasible for a Perfectionist to research even as they'll be being rigidly guided by a moralistic, youngsters voice, further they run the risk of being in reality immersed in it. They pay attention to it with diligence and cannot distinguish it from their grown-up self. The key step in a Perfectionist's direction towards boom is to learn how to be aware of the voice objectively and take from the best components at the equal time as distancing themselves from the horrific elements. A professional therapist want to be properly geared up to assist advantage this improvement – but first, a Perfectionist must advantage sufficient self-records to be inclined to are seeking out out their help.

The related sorts of the Perfectionist are:

Wing: Mediator nine

Wing: Giver 2

Security Type: Epicure 7

Stress Type: Romantic 4

The non-related, appearance-alike kinds of the Perfectionist are:

Performer 3

Loyal Skeptic 6

Protector eight

The Probability of types (different sorts to take into account if Perfectionist is your pinnacle preference):

66% Perfectionist 1

eight% Romantic four

eight% Loyal Skeptic 6

7% Giver 2

The 66% percent chance assigned to the Perfectionist type way that there can be a excessive danger you're a Perfectionist in case you scored the immoderate at the Perfectionist check. However, you want to however review your 2nd and zero.33 options and the alternative possibly sorts (Romantic and Loyal Skeptic. Givers are frequently the second and third sorts associated with the Perfectionist). Remember, if a amazing kind has a strong wing of 1 or the opportunity, that might significantly have an impact on how the character manifests itself. If you cannot acquire the type you're, your emotions can be legitimate, or can be a forestall quit result of the horrible stereotypes you have heard about the type, so make certain to find out any robust reactions you may have.

Myths About the Perfectionist:

If you are a perfectionist, you're frequently defined as an inflexible neat freak. You may additionally additionally will be predisposed to determine humans constant with excessive requirements, but the ones necessities can range. Thus, if a perfectionist takes vicinity to accept as true with that being neat is a waste of time, or that being flexible is a extraordinary feature, they may not show off some of those stereotypical developments.

Adjectives to Describe the Perfectionist:

In addition to the above, Perfectionists are seemed to have the terrible traits of being green with envy, essential and opinionated. They are associated with immoderate fine dispositions, along with being conscientious, having immoderate necessities, being clean, constant, self-controlled and unique.

The Underlying Truths of the Perfectionist

The simple precept the perfectionist has forgotten: All human beings are one and are best as they are.

The perfectionist wrongly believes: That we aren't time-venerated for who we are.

The Perfectionist maximum deeply fears: To be evil, faulty, corrupt or immoral.

The Perfectionist maximum deeply dreams: To be ethical, to be correct, to be complete and to have integrity.

The Perfectionist is most profoundly stimulated with the aid of way of using the ones dreams and desires: To constantly be proper, to keep aiming higher and improving the whole lot spherical them, to justify themselves, to be steady with their excessive beliefs, to be above reproach so that it will keep away from horrible judgment of any kind, regardless of how small, from all of us they meet.

The perfectionist created those behaviors to catch up on: Growing up in an surroundings wherein love modified into given out because of suitable behavior which includes being responsible and conscientious. In the case of warfare, they located out to swallow their anger, and as a give up stop end result, are full of anxiety and resentment.

The Characteristics that Define the Perfectionist

Because of those adaptive behaviors, the Perfectionist makes a speciality of: Judging what is proper and looking for to right any wrongs; comparing their conduct to others; criticizing themselves and others.

They positioned their energy into: Suppressing non-public needs and goals, retaining immoderate standards and being proper all the time.

They desperately try to keep away from: Mistakes, loss of self-control, any violation of social norms, dropping love because of "bad" conduct.

They have those strengths: Perfectionists have a immoderate diploma of integrity and are devoted to self-improvement. They display terrific self-restraint, contribute generously to efforts they deem essential, and exhibit idealism.

They communicate within the following way: Perfectionists are smooth and direct with black and white questioning. This effects in being perceived as being judgmental or closed-minded.

The Sources of Stress, Anger and Defensiveness

They are harassed through the use of: Because the Perfectionist has a strong inner critic, they are able to undergo a terrific deal of tension while they may be no longer able to near it off. In conditions where there is an exceptional huge shape of issues, the Perfectionist can have a tendency to freeze up. They can hold onto resentment, in particular at the equal time as others blame them and do not take responsibility for what is truely their mistake.

They are angered: When topics are finished within the wrong way, or at the same time as regulations are left out.

They are defensive within the direction of: Unfair complaint.

Their anger and defensiveness are characterised with the aid of: Repressed resentment blended with intense, self-righteous justification. This repressed resentment regularly floods out into outbursts of angry anger.

Their very last motive is: To take transport of that humans are inherently entire, entire and ideal as they may be and that their price is not counting on being proper.

Suggestions for Personal Growth for the Perfectionist

They can further this increase through:

•Being privy to methods they screen ethical behavior and appreciating that the severa perspectives of others may additionally imply that they behave in techniques that seem "incorrect."

•Letting skip of judgments.

•Practicing forgiveness of the self and of others.

•Questioning their internal tension on a each day foundation.

•Identifying repressed goals thru noticing wherein they hold resentment.

•Viewing desires and herbal impulses as high pleasant and integrating them into their lifestyles.

•Making nice to time desk unfastened time for the duration of which priorities can freely floor, at the side of longer get-away intervals.

•Getting real data to avoid unfounded worry. Learning the manner to request and to get hold of gratification.

Their biggest impediment is: A tendency within the route of being a workaholic, that is on account of this perception that they've to be suitable enough at the way to be loved.

Others can guide this growth via:

•Encouraging a perfectionist to spend time on self-care.

•Providing them with a compassionate perspective.

•Kindly looking and bringing up on the same time as the phrase "have to" seem of their speech.

Famous Perfectionists

(along with many philosophers, leaders, musicians, politicians, and actors):

Helen Hunt, Harrison Ford, Maggie Smith, William F. Buckley, Jerry Seinfeld, Keith Olbermann, Vanessa Redgrave, Julie Andrews, Emma Thompson, Meryl Streep, Tina Fey, Katherine Hepburn, George F. Will, Bill Moyers, Noam Chomsky, Osama bin Laden, George Bernard Shaw, Thoreau, Rudy Giuliani, Elliot Spitzer, Joan Baez, Celine Dion, Ralph Nader, Hilary Clinton, Justice Sandra Day O'Connor, Al Gore, Dr. Jack Kevorkian, Martha Stewart, Prince Charles, Duchess of Cambridge, Margaret

Thatcher, Jimmy Carter, Michelle Obama, Confucius, Plato, Joan of Arc, Sir Thomas More, Mahatma Gandhi, Pope John Paul II, and Nelson Mandela.

Related Types

Every personality type is stimulated with the useful resource of the wings to the factor that they'll combination into taken into consideration considered one of them. If a man or woman kind has a strong wing, it'll make a large impact at the person's character.

Wings: If you are a one with a more superior wing, you will be predisposed to be lots a great deal much less bloodless and additional beneficial. If you are a one with a extra superior 9 wing, you have a propensity to be plenty less warm, but additionally greater tranquil or even indifferent.

Security Type (Epicure 7): When a Perfectionist movements within the direction of the excessive satisfactory component of seven, they'll be able to be more accepting of themselves and others, experience life greater, and act with more spontaneity and pride. When a Perfectionist movements in the direction of the awful trouble of seven, they may lean inside the direction of substance abuse or one of a kind awful conduct.

Stress Type (Romantic four): When a Perfectionist movements in the direction of the powerful aspect of four, they're able to get proper of get admission to to their repressed feelings and access extra creativity. The horrible aspect of four can motive the Perfectionist to end up depressed and revel in hopeless approximately what they do now not have.

Overlaps Between the Perfectionist and Other Non-related Types

The Performer 3: The Performer and Perfectionist every location a immoderate cost on purpose-orientated sports activities

activities and proportion a tendency to vicinity art work often else. However, at the same time as the Perfectionist suffers due to a harsh inner critic, the Performer might possibly look for brief cuts a very good way to get earlier.

The Romantic 4: These two types are carefully related because of the fact the Perfectionist is the protection kind of the Romantic and the Romantic is the stress type of the Perfectionist. These kinds are both very expressive of idealism, further to a commitment to improving themselves. However, the Perfectionist is excellent due to the fact their idealism is all geared within the path of "getting it proper" but the Romantic is pushed via acquiring achievement. Another large difference has to do with the fact that Romantics can be self-absorbed and drown of their emotions. Perfectionists are, as an alternative, lots extra repressed.

The Loyal Skeptic 6: These kinds may be similar because of the truth both revel in excessive ranges of anxiety as they're attempting to understand the area spherical them. The vital difference is that the Loyal Skeptic over-analyzes in a look for safety on the identical time because the Perfectionist does so an brilliant way to keep away from horrible judgment.

The Protector 8: Both kinds belong to the frame center and, therefore, are centered on fact and justice. Whereas Protectors are comfortable venting their anger and short spring into motion, Perfectionists are masters at suppressing their anger until it in the end boils over.

The Mediator nine: Both kinds belong to the equal frame middle, that's why they have got hundreds in common. They each are resultseasily able to suppress their goals that allows you to get what they actually fee. Both types moreover rate regular and hard paintings. However, while

Perfectionists are inflexible in their ideals, Mediators are bendy (once in a while overly so).

Chapter 2: The Giver

Givers face a positive paradox in phrases of what it in truth manner to be a actual Giver. These people can be certainly useful to the human beings round them, but on the identical time as they're no longer simply healthy, they're obsessed on giving insofar as they need to be perceived as beneficial (whether or not or not or now not or now not they absolutely assist or maybe damage others). Givers thrive on looking for to go out in their manner to help others and on being abundantly beneficiant. For them, this is the maximum widespread, maximum precious way to experience regular lifestyles. Healthy Givers sense real undertaking for people and need to do right. Feeling love internal themselves allows them to spread greater like to others. It is likewise what makes them experience as though they're profitable. The type is within the principal concerned with love, intimacy, sharing with others, and nurturing own family, and near friendships.

A balanced and healthy Giver is able to be type, beneficial, generous, and aware about one of a kind people's need and goals. Other humans are interested in them in a way that feels almost magnetic. Balanced givers are capable of help others experience warmth definitely from their proximity. They have the triumphing of understanding a way to energize others via their devices (both fabric and non secular). They realize the way to shower wholesome hobby and appreciation on their loved ones, and the way to help them to apprehend the most top notch tendencies in themselves that possibly have been ignored. Basically, healthful Givers are the archetype of the proper discern that each infant goals of. They are capable of see others of their truest state, to comprehend them with out a shred of judgment, and in no way appears to be quick on staying power. As their call shows, the Giver is constantly satisfied to increase a assisting hand. They moreover percentage the excellent capability to recognize exactly how and at the same time as to permit skip – like a figure helping a more youthful little one discover ways to journey a bicycle with out schooling wheels. The actual gift of the Healthy Twos is they understand the manner to open the hearts of even the maximum repressed person. Their ears are already so open that their instance teaches us the way to be more thoroughly and complexly human.

The difficulty that the Giver faces is available in phrases in their inner development. The darkish side of the Giver that can limit their inner improvement consists of pride, deception of themselves and of others, and a loss of limitations. The Giver would likely experience the not possible to withstand need to come to be too involved in specific humans's lives. This ought to likely redecorate into the bad dependancy of really working to govern extraordinary humans if you want to get their non-public emotional desires met. It is critical to explore the ones dark locations with a view to effect actual transformation. However, the Giver does no longer want to well known such darkish places in themselves because it contradicts their enjoy of self as honestly fantastic, even idealized to the element of sainthood.

This want to face a worry of worthlessness is really the largest obstacle dealing with Givers (similarly to Types Three and Types Four). All 3 types venture an outward image of self notion. However, underneath the floor, they all worry that they have no intrinsic fee in themselves and, therefore, they want to be or to perform a little aspect above and beyond, if they'll be to win love and reputation from others. When Givers are veering towards the damaging realm in their personalities, they art work to cultivate a misleading photo of being really unselfish, self-sacrificing and generous. They act as despite the reality that they do now not need any shape of gratification for themselves. This is opposite to the fact, which is they regularly have very excessive and unrealistic expectations, coupled with unacknowledged emotional needs.

When a Giver veers toward the horrific prevent of the spectrum, they are insatiable of their want to are searching for validation. Under the tutelage of their superego's desires, they sacrifice the whole thing they will with a purpose to make awesome people love them. When they positioned other human beings earlier than themselves and act loving and unselfish, they expect that routinely makes them entitled to unconditional love. Unfortunately, after they continuously located others first, they sincerely become secretly irritated and envious. These emotions contradict their identity as Giver, in order that they work diligently to repress them. Inevitably, the Giver will erupt, whether or not or not through an emotional outburst which can even appear to be a infantile tantrum or thru greater diffused passive-competitive behaviors. These outbursts generally will be predisposed to do high-quality harm to the Givers' relationships, as it threatens to find the genuine motives for their beneficiant, loving behavior, which makes them appear inauthentic to their loved ones.

The linked styles of the Giver are:

Wing: Perfectionist 1

Wing: Performer three

Security Type: Romantic four

Stress Type: Protector 8

The non-linked, look-alike sorts of the Giver are:

Epicure 7

Mediator nine

The danger of kinds (differing types to remember if Giver is your pinnacle preference):

sixty five% Giver

8% Epicure

eight% Mediator

7% Romantic

5% Perfectionist

The 65% percent hazard assigned to the Giver kind approach that there is a excessive threat you're a Giver if you acquired a excessive score. However, you need to nevertheless assessment whether or now not your 2d and 1/3 picks in form the other probably sorts (Epicure, Mediator, Romantic and Perfectionist). Remember, if a sure type has a sturdy wing of 1 or the opportunity, which could extensively impact how the persona manifests itself. If you cannot be given the sort you're, your emotions can be legitimate, or may be a result of the bad stereotypes you've got were given have been given heard about the type, so make certain to discover any robust reactions you can have.

Myths About the Giver

The Giver has a horrible popularity of giving due to the truth she or he has an ulterior reason: To get something in cross back. Givers also are associated with being primarily based, or perhaps needy.

Adjectives that Describe the Giver

The best adjectives encompass: Responsible, insightful, bendy, positive, generous, loving, kind, sensitive to human beings's feelings, and nurturing. The horrible adjectives encompass: Indirect, overly proud, intrusive, hysterical, and dramatic.

The Underlying Truths of the Giver

The essential principle the giver has forgotten: That the dreams of anybody are manifestly met inside the universe's go along with the go with the flow of giving and receiving.

The giver wrongly believes: The great manner to get is to provide and the most effective manner to be loved is through being favored.

The giver created the ones behaviors to compensate: In order to get their dreams met, the Giver tried to make themselves crucial, overlooking their non-public needs and wants.

The Characteristics that Define the Giver

Because of those adaptive behaviors, the Giver focuses on: First and principal, one-of-a-type humans and relationships, at the cost of their very private non-public identity.

They positioned their electricity into: Figuring out what human beings want and want and looking to anticipate their dreams. Finding and preserving romantic relationships. Keeping the respect and incredible reward of various people.

They desperately try and avoid: Rejection, disappointment, a lack of appreciation and the possibility of being discarded.

They have these strengths: They are generous, giving and beneficial. They are sensitive to extraordinary people's want and goals. They are continuously expressive in their appreciation of others. They are supportive and fantastically energetic.

They speak in the following way: The Giver is expressive and beneficiant in giving advice to cherished ones. This style would possibly seem intrusive, but it can additionally be pleasant and useful.

The Sources of Stress, Anger and Defensiveness

They are forced through: Being pulled in all forms of instructions primarily based on their insatiable need to provide, no longer information their actual desires, and having their needs unmet.

They are angered about: Constantly feeling like their wishes aren't being met.

They are shielding closer to: Feeling unappreciated or controlled with the aid of the use of others

Their anger and defensiveness are characterized as such: Via unpredictable outbursts that appear uncharacteristic. Outburst ought to probably encompass tears and accusations thrown towards loved ones.

Personal Growth

Their very last goal is: To begin to recognize that the vital issue in phrases of being cherished is being themselves, and that giving and receiving is part of the natural flow of the universe.

They can in addition this growth thru:

•Understanding what unconditional love is.

•Identifying the want to flatter others and reap approval.

•Recognizing their personal goals in region of focusing at the desires of others.

•Trying now not to be really every person's "super pal."

•Being attentive on the equal time as trying to be beneficial may additionally seem like controlling.

•Identifying their private limits so that they do not burn out.

Their largest obstacle is: Guilt. This would possibly get up itself in terms of horrific feelings that rise up even as the Giver tries to fulfill his or her very very very own dreams. The Giver is further blocked via constantly searching for to rationalize what wishes to be completed for others in advance than doing subjects for themselves. Even even as the Giver is offered a few thing, he or she is in all likelihood to refuse it, regardless of the reality that it's far what they really want.

Others can assist this boom via manner of:

•Appreciating the Giver themselves, in place of turning into depending on what she or he has to provide.

•Checking in regularly on what they want and want.

•Regularly saying thank you and specially telling them precisely what you understand approximately them.

•Taking an interest of their problems, despite the truth that they may be seeking to keep away from talking approximately them

•being slight with grievance.

•Reassuring them approximately your feelings.

•Encouraging them to say no, set limits and positioned into effect boundaries.

Famous Givers

(along facet many actors, musicians and philanthropists):

Priscilla Presley, Leo Buscaglia, Dolly Parton, Danny Thomas, Luciano Pavarotti, Monica Lewinsky, Nancy Reagan, Richard Thomas "John Boy Walton," Jennifer Tilly, Kenny G, Martin Sheen, Josh Groban, Eleanor Roosevelt, Barry Manilow, Juliette Binoche, Bobby McFerrin, Richard Simmons, John Denver, Ann Landers, Paula Abdul, Arsenio Hall, Pope John XXIII, Byron Katie, Bishop Desmond Tutu, Lionel Richie, Stevie Wonder, Music of Journey, Elizabeth Taylor, and Danny Glover.

Related Types

Every character type is inspired thru the wings to the element that they could blend into truely one of them. If a character type has a strong wing, it'll make a huge impact at the character's persona.

Perfectionist 1 (wing): When a Giver has a more potent Perfectionist wing, they'll be more idealistic, goal and judgmental. The kinds have similarly excessive requirements and might cognizance intensively at the health of others. They are every masterful at suppressing their dreams. However, even as Perfectionists attempt to decorate others based totally totally on their inner, inflexible standards, the Giver will change him or herself to make the opposite person satisfied.

Performer three (wing): These kinds are doubly related because of the fact they belong to the equal Heart Center kind, which reasons them to percentage tremendous individual tendencies. Givers and Performers each will be inclined to be "doers" who are complete of power and keen to get things executed. They percentage a immoderate degree of power and a willingness to conform to 3 issue situation. These types are one-of-a-type due to the truth Givers are continually considering exceptional people's need and desires, even as Performers are so reason on getting topics finished that, they may disregard remarkable human beings's emotions. When a Giver has a stronger Performer wing, they'll be greater self-assured, ambitious and aggressive.

Romantic four (safety type): These sorts are doubly associated because they belong to the identical Heart Center type, which motives them to percent excessive best character inclinations. (Note, the Giver is the stress form of the Romantic). These two types are very keyed in to extremely good people's emotions. They can be overly touchy and are very devoted to their relationships. Their immoderate diploma of emotional depth can make them quality romantic companions and gifted artists. Their critical distinction is that Givers are extra focused on out of doors factors, at the same time as Romantics usually will be inclined to appearance internal and can will be inclined inside the course of melancholy. When a Giver actions closer to the superb thing of four, they are able to famend their bad emotions and locate new assets of self-price other than supporting others. When they skip to the terrible thing of 4, they'll be even extra judgmental of themselves as compared to others and tend in the course of self-absorption and despair.

Protector 8 (stress kind): These kinds are carefully related due to the fact the Giver is the protection form of the Protector and the Protector is the pressure type of the Giver. These kinds also are similar because of the reality they every have lively personalities that typically normally have a tendency in the path of generosity and protectiveness. Both sorts are attracted to electricity. However, at the equal time as Givers use this electricity to assist humans, protectors use their energy inside the form of manner that would virtually scare others for his or her very very own gain and enjoy of right and wrong. When a Giver movements to the superb component of the Protector, they are capable of experience extra confident, which lets in them extra really. They prevent disturbing plenty about what unique people think about them. When a Giver actions within the route of the poor aspect of the Protector, they lose their loving nature and turn irritable. They can isolate themselves and begin making wishes on other humans. They could possibly even grow to be controlling inside the path of various human beings.

Overlaps Between the Giver and Other Non-related Types

Epicure 7: The Epicure is much like the Giver because of their shared lively attitudes. They are human beings pleasers who can also additionally also be seductive in their behaviors closer to others. They range because Epicures want to interest on themselves and what they need and may with out troubles emerge as self-absorbed. The Giver, alternatively, is constantly focused on other people and smooth to sacrifice his or her experience of self.

Mediator nine: Givers and Mediators are every people pleasers who can lose their personal revel in of self in pursuit of feeling wanted. Givers try this greater actively, searching out approval, at the same time as Mediators do that reactively, as they'll be pulled among competing forces. Givers can be too intrusive, whilst Mediators are not intrusive the least bit.

Chapter 3: The Performer

When the Performer is at their satisfactory, they may be primed to perform some of the great achievements feasible for mankind. They are the jewels of humanity and, as such, they'll be often the supply of tremendous admiration at the a part of others—not only due to their non-public achievements, but because of their kind and gracious way. Balanced Performers apprehend how suitable it is able to enjoy to preserve on improving themselves so that you can stretch in the direction of extra accomplishments. They thrive whilst they may be able to contribute their superb skills to the society round them. Better but, additionally they recognize being capable of encourage exceptional people to be the brilliant possible version of themselves that they may be. The Performer is someone who has an inclination to be nicely favored or even well-known amongst their pals. They would be the pupil that is frequently elected "class president" or "home coming queen" due to the reality their high-quality electricity makes people need to partner with them—even to the detail of using them as a private avatar. A wholesome performer is capable of encompass the whole lot this is the superb in a given way of lifestyles. This method that others are capable of see their aspirations and desires reflected in their photo.

Like a confident actor, Performers in truth trust in themselves and count on that they have to develop themselves into even better variations of the humans that they're. This makes them the most a success and nicely preferred of all the kinds, in popular. Healthy Performers can characteristic a living, breathing feature version because of the reality they're able to encompass socially valued traits to an top notch degree. Because healthy Performers absolutely keep in mind they may be nicely really worth the strive that it'd take to end up the best that they will be. They are frequently successful in obtaining their dreams. When things are going nicely and working in line with nature, their outstanding achievement can artwork to encourage the people round them to invest greater in their non-public self- care and self- improvement.

A Performer is relentless of their pursuit of success. That experience of success is determined not through the usage of a few intrinsic belief, as inside the case of the Perfectionist discussed above. Their belief of achievement comes from out of doors sources, whether or not it's far defined thru their family, their way of life, and their social setting. This have to mean in search of to acquire the most high-priced fabric possessions and financial recognition symbols, which incorporates the maximum important house, the fattest pockets or the flashiest automobile. It may also propose reaching wonderful varieties of achievement, for example, inside the realm of expertise. If they arrive from an academic family, they will attempt to distinguish themselves in a college setting or in a systematic laboratory. Often, due to the truth the call shows, the Performer desires to become famous, whether or not or not as an actor, a style model, an artist, writer or public discern. Performers often are politicians, comedians or precise sorts of public audio machine. In a religious family, this could appear itself in phrases of encouragement to come to be a community chief, whether or not or now not it's far a minister, a priest, or a rabbi, professions that every one carry a certain reputation. Regardless of the manner every Performer is acquainted with achievement, they may constantly attempt to benefit recognition. The worst thing that could arise to a Performer is that they revel in like they're a no person.

Because of those compulsions, Performers have a take a look at as kids to behave in techniques that earn them powerful hobby and phrases of reward from the adults round them—they may grow to be specifically related to any grownup who lavishes the most excessive phrases upon them, whether or not or no longer they will be honest. Whatever activities look like recognized as maximum valuable through their social circle are the matters that Performers maximum want to do, and they located a apparently endless quantity of electricity into excelling at those subjects. Performers also have a look at as youngsters a manner to assist and expand a few aspect approximately them receives be conscious from legitimate contributors in their community.

While it is in fact real that each one people need love, attention, manual, and the confirmation in their self-worth if you want to sincerely thrive, the Performer is truly the type that most exemplifies this normal social stress. The Performer does now not need success due to what it may allow them to shop for (like sevens), nor for the strength and feeling of independence that they desire it will supply (like eights). Instead, they actually desire achievement because of the truth they will be afraid that without it, they'll be destined to vanish into an abyss of nothingness and worthlessness. Performers experience that they're no individual, until they accumulate the burst of first-rate hobby delivered by way of the usage of the use of fulfillment and accomplishment.

This is likewise in which the Performers run into their worst deliver of problem. Because they will do some thing on the way to accomplish the difficulty that ensures to guide them to sense a higher feel of self esteem, the Performer faces a sincere risk of turning into alienated—even to the thing that they lose any revel in in their proper identification and motive, their actual emotions and their actual pastimes. When they'll be on this unbalanced state, it is easy to misinform a Performer, letting them without trouble fall prey to scams and con artists. Beyond all of this risk, the Performer truely faces a deeper trouble, it's far the reality that their look for a manner to be of truly well worth permits form a vicious downwards spiral, as it keeps to take them further and in addition faraway from their non-public proper self wherein their core of real price is residing. This gadget typically begins for the duration of their children years even as the Performer starts offevolved offevolved to come to be depending on receiving hobby from the ones spherical them and in embracing the characteristics rewarded via others. This reasons them to step by step lose touch with themselves, which typically manifests itself in a few unspecified time inside the destiny in their teenage rebellious years. The greater they encompass the inclinations valued by way of way of manner of others, the extra they go away inside the returned in their real, internal self, until in the destiny they awaken and recognize they do not even recognize who that self is or a manner to assist it.

Because of this sluggish experience of loss, the Performer is a paradoxical type. Although they're the number one kind inside the Heart Center, the Performer isn't always taken into consideration by means of others to be a "feeling" character. Instead, they may be continuously appeared to be people of relentless motion and fulfillment. This is possibly due to the reality they positioned their emotions away in a location so that it will allow themselves to try to get earlier with what they may be aiming to reap in lifestyles. The Performer is so dedicated to their usual usual overall performance that they may be willing to suppress their emotions that they view as an impediment. In the vicinity of emotions, they embody wondering and practical actions.

The Performer regularly has problem on the same time as a person makes them renowned how an awful lot they've got shaped their lives to the expectancies of diverse human beings. They frequently have trouble taking the subsequent soar ahead to understand what they absolutely want because of the fact they regularly absolutely haven't any concept. Even even though it is a very common question, it modified into now not one that they remembered ever tackling earlier than. With all of this in thoughts, we are capable to say that the underlying problem that the dangerous Performer faces is that they have no longer been given permission to attempt to be who they actually are and, therefore, they have got repressed their private actual characteristics. As younger kids, they were over and over given the message that they could not own disruptive emotions and genuinely be themselves. Acceptance satisfactory got here when they had been able to positioned on the socially prescribed mask. This, of direction, is a primary trouble faced via manner of all individuals of society. However, due to the unique heritage and makeup of the Performer, they may be surprisingly vulnerable to those messages. They live and breathe them till they take shipping of them as their unquestioned, unquestionable truth. Fortunately, however, this want to human beings please way that Performers may be a lot less hard to steer to simply take delivery of help than differing types; whether or no longer they'll be capable of in fact do the important artwork to clearly accumulate happiness is an open query.

The associated types of the Performer are:

Wing: Giver 2

Wing: Romantic 4

Security Type: Loyal Skeptic 6

Stress Type: Mediator nine

The maximum not unusual non-linked forms of the Performer are:

Epicure 7

Perfectionist 1

Protector 8

The hazard of types (differing types to maintain in mind if Performer is your top choice):

fifty four% Performer 3

thirteen% Epicure 7

nine% Perfectionist 1

7% Giver 2

5% Protector 8

5% Mediator 9

If you scored excessive on the Performer test, you've got a 54% possibility that that is your kind. However, you must are seeking recommendation out of your 2d and 1/3 pinnacle rankings to look if you is probably an Epicure, Perfectionist, Giver, Protector or Mediator as the ones types can often be pressured. Remember, if a pleasant type has a sturdy wing of 1 or the other, that can significantly effect how the persona manifests itself. If you can not take delivery of the sort you're, your feelings can be legitimate, or may be a stop end result of the horrible stereotypes you've got heard approximately the type, so make certain to find out any robust reactions you can have.

Myths About the Performer

The maximum horrible stereotypes approximately the Performer is that they're self-absorbed, egotistical and bored with different people, but they can be very being involved and are complete of initiative— which includes supporting others. The Performer can be seen as misleading, but they do no longer lie to an amazing manner to damage different people because of the reality they're unsure of their real identity and because of this regularly shift their behaviors as they look for it.

Adjectives used for the Performer

Optimistic, lively, confident, enthusiastic, industrious, realistic, grounded and speedy-paced are the extraordinary adjectives. Impatient, rushed, self-aggrandizing, vindictive, useless, superficial, workaholic pretentious and aggressive are the terrible adjectives.

The Underlying Truths of the Performer

The number one precept the Performer has forgotten: Natural legal tips will permit all matters to art work as they want to.

The Performer wrongly believes: It is essential to avoid failure the least bit charges. All humans want to work on my own and for themselves. Rewards come way to movements not identity.

The Performer created those behaviors to compensate: Working for approval in case you need to experience cherished and, for that reason, shielding their actual goals and desires.

The Characteristics that Define the Performer

Because of those adaptive behaviors, the perfectionist specializes in: Getting matters finished, being the excellent normally, being the maximum inexperienced person viable.

They located their electricity into: Accomplishing dreams, staying busy, getting popularity for his or her accomplishments, self-promoting and searching as actual as feasible.

They desperately try to keep away from: Failure, embarrassment, uncomfortable emotions, displaying doubt, slowing down and being incapable of doing subjects.

They have those strengths: Being an enthusiastic, capable, well desired chief. Being sensible, inspirational and prepare.

They speak inside the following way: With direct, clean to apprehend language that could veer into impatience or insensitivity.

The Sources of Stress, Anger and Defensiveness

They are pressured with the beneficial aid of: All the strain to commonly get subjects executed, reap greater, and acquire a higher recognition and fee; the priority of failure.

They are angered approximately: Anything that gets of their manner, together with incompetent and inefficient human beings.

They are defensive toward: Criticism from others, specifically the ones they do no longer recognize pretty.

Their anger and defensiveness are characterised as such: Occasional irritable outbursts, frequent signs and symptoms and symptoms of impatience.

Personal Growth

Their very last purpose is: To receive being loved no matter their achievements.

They can in addition this growth with the aid of using:

•Being conscious after they postpone emotions ("I'll be satisfied at the same time as…").

•Taking gain in their natural resilience, optimism and versatility.

Their largest obstacle is:

•Avoiding ordinary comparisons with others.

•Feeling like they continuously need to perform.

•Not reacting aggressively when they hit upon incompetent behavior in others.

•Knowing while to prevent.

•Noticing while fantasies of fulfillment become greater vital than actual skills.

Others can help this boom via:

•Helping them recognize limits and leaving time for their feelings to floor earlier than they run off to perform the subsequent undertaking on their listing.

•Keeping them grounded and not ruled by way of way of the usage of myth.

•Providing guide in making alternatives based definitely totally on emotions rather than choice for reputation.

•Reminding them they are loved for who they're no longer for what they do.

•Discouraging comparisons among them and others.

•Allowing them to have down time and no longer continuously revel in like they ought to perform.

Famous Performers

(collectively with a number of the most influential politicians, audio system and actors, however furthermore a few infamous, duplicitous criminals):

Oprah Winfrey, Bill Clinton, Deepak Chopra, O.J. Simpson, Michael Jordan, Paul McCartney, Elvis Presley, Will Smith, Courtney Cox, Jon Bon Jovi, Bernie Madoff, John Edwards, Taylor Swift, Tiger Woods, Ken Watanabe, Richard Gere, Justin Bieber, Truman Capote, Emperor Constantine, Madonna, Ben Kingsley, Demi Moore, Lance Armstrong, Jamie Foxx, Andy Warhol, Tony Robbins, Barbra Streisand, Augustus Caesar, Tony Blair, Prince William, Arnold Schwarzenegger, Carl Lewis, Muhammed Ali, Mitt Romney, Bill Wilson (AA Founder), Whitney Houston, Lady Gaga, Brooke Shields, Cindy Crawford, Tom Cruise, Kevin Spacey and Anne Hathaway.

Related Types

Every man or woman type is precipitated by means of manner of the wings to the thing that they might blend into taken into consideration one in every of them. If a character type has a robust wing, it'll make a huge effect at the individual's character.

Giver 2 (wing): When a Performer has a more advanced 2 wing, they may be seductive, sociable and famous. These types are even more intently associated than different sorts because of the fact they belong to the identical Heart Center kind, which reasons them to percentage certain character traits. Because Givers and Performers each have a propensity to be "doers," they'll be full of power and eager to get things finished. They percentage a excessive diploma of power and a willingness to comply to some thing they face. These sorts variety because of the fact Performers are greater cause on getting subjects carried out at the same time as

Givers are continuously thinking about distinct human beings's want and desires.

Romantic 4 (wing): When a Performer has a extra advanced four wing, they will be introspective, creative and pretentious. The Romantic and the Performer are even extra carefully related than amazing associated kinds because of the truth they proportion the equal Heart Center types. They each are enthusiastic about getting special human beings's approval and popularity. Their excessive creativity allows them of their artwork, however they both may be aggressive. Their differences are that Performers are always centered on a future purpose on the identical time as Romantics are a great deal less so while you recall that they may be often distracted by way of way of their inner attention.

Loyal Skeptic 6 (safety kind): These types are intently related due to the truth the Performer is the pressure form of the Loyal Skeptic and the Loyal Skeptic is the protection shape of the Performer. Both sorts proportion a pleasing, humans fascinating personality despite the truth that Performers tend to be more stable and trusting once they circulate inside the course of sixes whilst Loyal Skeptics in strain become extra energetic and eager to fulfill their goals. On the superb aspect, while a Performer movements toward six, they grow to be more familial and group oriented in addition to prone and emotionally on hand (in an incredible way). On the lousy component, they may be extra terrified of rejection, and greater annoying and indecisive.

Mediator nine (strain kind): On the brilliant trouble, at the identical time as a Performer moves in the direction of 9, they'll be greater snug and peaceful and receptive. They can advantage a better mind-set on life. On the terrible component, at the equal time as a Performer actions towards nine, they may be capable of procrastinate, become apathetic and forget approximately themselves to the element of great harm.

Overlaps among the Performer and distinct non-related kinds

The Perfectionist 1: These types every place a excessive charge on purpose-oriented sports activities and proportion a bent to place artwork specially else. However, at the same time as the Perfectionist suffers because of a harsh internal critic, the Performer could possibly look for short cuts so that you can get in advance.

The Epicure 7: The similarities most of the ones types derive from the truth that both are energetic and energetic—and regularly too busy. Both like to avoid horrible emotions, which incorporates unhappiness. Their crucial distinction comes from the reality that at the same time as Epicures sense entitled to their private fitness, Performers are driven through manner of a revel in of social approval. Performers are inquisitive about being green, on the identical time as Epicures care more for pleasure.

The Protector 8: Performers and Protectors are comparable due to the truth both are assertive and movement-oriented. Both are herbal leaders who aren't afraid to step on a person who receives of their manner. The most important distinction is that at the same time as Protectors can be confrontational and connected to their function, Performers can be angered while someone gets in the way in their achievement.

Chapter 4: The Romantic

When you bear in mind the Romantic, you need to now not don't forget contemporary-day romantic comedies, however alternatively the ancient decide of the romantic artist, typically a poet or a musician who become basically high-quality from others – which changed into each the deliver of genius and of profound struggling and isolation. The Romantic has the sensation that they'll be specific from all one-of-a-kind humans, and because of this, no character will ever be able to understand them or love them as lots as they desire. They often see themselves as uniquely proficient—and this is usually the case. While they will experience as though they have particular, one-of-a-kind offers, but moreover as singularly disadvantaged or imperfect. Romantics are the kind which is probably maximum touchy to and concerned via manner of what they apprehend as their personal inadequacies and deficiencies.

When healthful, a Romantic is honest and right of their innermost mind. When they have tough emotions, they haven't any trouble proudly proudly owning as lots as them, questioning their motives, and reading any contradictions. The maximum excessive of emotional conflicts will do nothing to phase them. They can stare them inside the face at the same time as not having to deny or lessen them. They aren't blind and might not always like what they locate, but no matter how painful it is probably, they do not try to justify their problems, blame them on one-of-a-type people, or attempt to disguise them from themselves or the ones round them. They aren't afraid to appearance themselves within the mirror and be aware every unsightly a part of themselves. When they may be healthful, the Romantics are open approximately sharing every part of themselves, which include quite private reminiscences and probable embarrassing records. They do that at splendid personal chance because of the truth they see the gain of coming to recognize the fact of their enjoy, fine and awful alike. They recognise that the fine way to increase and change is mastering thru mistakes and coming to phrases with private luggage, regardless of how cumbersome and heavy. This ability moreover enables the Romantic with the intention to go through suffering with a quiet, dignified electricity. Their intimate know-how with their non-public darker side makes it less complicated for them to method any painful memories that might threaten to destabilize the opportunity eight sorts.

Despite the apparent advantages that come from such an outlook on existence, the Romantic does now not have the whole thing all discovered. In reality, the Romantic regularly opinions that they have the sensation that some thing is lacking deep inner of themselves, however they often have first rate trouble looking to pick out

out exactly what that some component is. It is probably features collectively with social adeptness, will electricity, self-self notion or maybe emotional tranquility. These are developments that they generally see in everyone however themselves, and frequently in an tremendous supply. Thanks to their very astute and unflinching nature, however, with time and enough attitude, the Romantic can normally be made to recognize that this isn't a question of an aim lack on their issue. Instead, they come to apprehend that they're honestly insecure approximately factors in their self-image, both in phrases of their character or their psyche. Once they recognize that they undergo due to this perceived lack of a smooth and sturdy identification—most significantly a social personality that they sense comfortable with—the Romantic is usually nicely on the street to carrying out their most self-expression.

Even despite the fact that the Romantic regularly feels one-of-a-type from exclusive people, it does now not advise that they revel in this solitude and isolation. In reality, any ostentatious demonstration of "taking issue in" loneliness on the a part of a Romantic might be an complicated defense mechanism built so that you can avoid the opportunity of rejection. They do no longer actually need to be on my own for prolonged intervals of time. Although they will experience socially awkward or uncomfortable, there may be absolute confidence that they profoundly choice to hook up with specific people who recognize them and all their maximum excessive feelings. The Romantic's dream is for a person to enter into their worlds and comprehend a manner to realize the innermost self that they have privately cultivated outside the general public sphere. The problem takes location even as, over the route of months or years, such recognition never comes. If that is the case, then the Romantic receives overly invested in having an identity targeted spherical how certainly one in all a type from anyone else they're. Therefore, the Romantic attempts to make him or herself revel in a whole lot less wounded by using the usage of the use of insisting on their identification as an insistent individualist. This can spill over proper right into a borderline detrimental insistence that they have got to do every single component on their non-public, in their very very personal manner, on their non-public unique phrases. Even in spite of the truth that they choice that they could in fact be like all and sundry else and percentage all of the self assurance and ease that maximum humans seem to expose off, they suffer in silence and that they undertake the chant of "I am myself. Nobody is acquainted with me. I am special and specific."

When a Romantic starts offevolved to get out of balance, the maximum most important symptom are signs and symptoms and signs of low shallowness and a bad self-picture. When the ones come to be continual, they may veer into melancholy or perhaps a detachment from reality. The Romantic tries to make up for this thru developing a personal avatar, which is basically an idealized version of themselves that has all the trends they lack. The problem is that this avatar can emerge as a deliver of terrible assessment and a completely creative Romantic can clearly start to revel in competitive, jealous or maybe greater insufficient in evaluation to this fantasy avatar decide.

The Romantic is one of the types that may go through the maximum shifts all through the path in their lives. They may moreover adopt numerous excellent identities, developing them on the patterns, the possibilities, or the traits they find out most attractive in different humans. However, underneath the reputedly audacious floor, they despite the fact that sense uncertain approximately the individual that they without a doubt are. The actual hassle stems from the truth that the Romantic continually bases their identity on their inconstant emotions. Thus, even as the Romantic seems inward, the reality that they're so emotionally astute method they may be able to see the real sort of human feelings. Rather than seeing secure identification, they see a kaleidoscope that continues moving. This capability, to successfully apprehend the reality approximately the dynamic exceptional of human nature, is a exceptional benefit. However, due to the reality they'll be driven to attempt to create a stable, reliable identity from their emotions, they always want to try and domesticate best a pick out few in their emotions while rejecting and suppressing others, which goes to build up anxiety over time. They play a little recreation internally in which they distinguish a few feelings as a part of themselves and specific emotions as not part of themselves. This workout, however small it appears, is truely a brilliant supply of struggling. When they connect to nice moods to select out with, they enjoy like they're being actual to themselves, on the equal time as they are in fact honestly excellent being real to a small part of their whole being.

Another hassle that the Romantic faces comes after they want to detach from the past, in particular, beyond lousy feelings. The Romantic is the type that maximum holds at once to horrible emotions about different humans, nursing their wounds manner longer than all of us else. These terrible emotions occupy the form of huge element inside the psyche of the Romantic (who's very skilled at visualizing them to the point that they appear real). For this motive, the Romantic runs the risk of having so related to nostalgic emotions of longing and disappointment that they emerge as not capable of see the many treasures proper earlier than their very non-public eyes.

Until the Romantic we could bypass of the notion that there may be some element essentially incorrect with them, they may in no way be able to permit themselves to experience or revel in their countless actual features. If they were to widely known their specific tendencies, they may end up losing their terrific experience of identification (as a suffering victim). When a Romantic is capable of learn how to see that masses in their inner narrative is not without a doubt actual, the ones antique emotions can begin to fall away. Then they will be eventually capable of prevent telling themselves their antique tale, which has become beside the factor to who they'll be proper now.

The related sorts of the Romantic are:

Wing: Performer 3

Wing: Observer five

Security Type: Perfectionist 1

Stress Type: Giver 2

The maximum commonplace, non-associated appearance-alike sorts of the Romantic are:

Loyal Skeptic 6

Mediator nine

Epicure 7

The opportunity of types (different sorts to hold in mind if Romantic is your top desire):

sixty one% Romantic 4

eleven% Perfectionist 2

7% dependable skeptic 6

7% mediator 9

five% epicure 7

Because of the sixty one% opportunity assigned to the Romantic, in case you scored immoderate on the Romantic check, there may be a amazing threat that this is your correct kind. There is also a smaller risk which you are without a doubt a Perfectionist, a Loyal Skeptic, a Mediator or an Epicure, so take a look at your 2d and 1/3 exquisite rankings to appearance in the event that they overlap, after which seek advice from the final segment of the financial ruin for critical distinguishing talents. Remember, if a amazing kind has a sturdy wing of one or the other, that would substantially affect how the character manifests itself. If you cannot receive the type you are, your emotions can be valid, or could be a end result of the bad stereotypes you've got got heard approximately the kind, so make sure to discover any strong reactions you can have.

Myths About the Romantic

The negative myths approximately the Romantic is that they're managed with the aid of their feelings and, consequently, can't be trusted. Nonetheless, Romantics absolutely are pretty steady and understand a way to get topics completed—if they're doing what they choose. They are known for making even the maximum mundane activities revel in precise.

Adjectives that Describe the Romantic

Creative, introspective, dramatic, idealistic, extreme, traumatic, empathetic, moody, self- absorbed, moralistic, depressed and cussed.

The Underlying Truths of the Romantic

The simple precept the Romantic has forgotten: All matters are deeply and absolutely connected to the whole thing else through their center.

The Romantic wrongly believes: They were abandoned and absence some thing that each one others have; they have no private identification or which means that within the international.

The Romantic created these behaviors to compensate: Because they're uncertain of themselves and their individuality, they try to make and surround themselves with stunning subjects. They will perform a little thing to maintain a given temper or sensation, and they may absolutely withdraw so you can defend their self-image and to take care of their emotional desires particularly else. Romantics have the addiction of attracting a "rescuer" who may not have their extraordinary pursuits at heart.

Myths About the Romantic

Romantics are criticized for being moody and self-conscious, for withholding themselves from others due to feelings of vulnerability and inadequacy. They on occasion are seen as feeling above anybody else and performing disdainful towards all but a delegated elite group of perceived equals. Romantics are visible as rule-breakers who assume that their particular developments make them exempt from ordinary procedures of residing. Like the stereotypical "romantic artist," fours are considered to suffer from troubles of self-indulgence, self-pity, and depression—even falling into despair.

Adjectives that Describe the Romantic

Romantics are frequently defined as self-conscious, touchy, and reserved. On the exceptional issue, they seem stimulated and clearly modern, and they are with out problems able to renew themselves and rework their opinions. They are frequently taken into consideration to be emotionally honest, modern, and in contact with the personal elements in their psyche. On the horrible period, they also can be moody and self-aware, melancholy, self-indulgent, and self-pitying.

The Characteristics that Define the Romantic

Because of these adaptive behaviors, the Romantic focuses on: What is right approximately the destiny and approximately the past; but additionally, what is missing them. They furthermore awareness on aesthetics and emotions, on the same time as frequently overlooking the existing second and the everyday subjects spherical them.

They positioned their energy into: All forms of immoderate emotions which might be all geared towards solving what's missing of their lifestyles. They often search for romantic connection, good sized fulfillment and looking for to be authentically specific.

They desperately attempt to keep away from: Rejection, abandonment, being omitted or belittled. Not being sufficient for precise people. Routines, ordinary every day life, and superficial human beings and sports activities activities.

They have the ones strengths: The Romantic is idea for their creativity basically, and their sensitivity. They are passionate, intense, idealistic and emotionally deep. They are expert at searching deep internal themselves and keying themselves into the emotions of others.

They talk within the following manner: By that specialize in themselves and their emotions, to the factor that they may come off as excessive, self-absorbed and difficult to satisfy.

The Sources of Stress, Anger and Defensiveness

They are burdened via: Anyone or some component that falls quick in their very excessive ideals. The perception that someone is more particular. The feeling that they in no manner have enough. Feelings that flow into past their normal (excessive) degree of depth.

They are angered approximately: Being disenchanted by way of way of others; false behavior at the a part of others; being seen as regular or now not particular.

They are protecting within the direction of: Being rejected or unconsidered.

Their anger and defensiveness are characterized as such: With depression, on the one hand, and with fiery outbursts of emotion or perhaps crying, as a substitute.

Personal Growth

Their very last goal is: To find out who they will be and what their significance is by using manner of the usage of developing a concrete, grounded non-public identification.

They can similarly this growth by means of: Mourning loss so that you can be able to skip beyond it, putting off self-sabotaging behaviors and finishing project, that specialize in what is ideal in area of what's missing.

Their largest impediment is: The manner their robust emotions can get in the manner of permitting them to take the popular movement. Their self-absorbed nature. Their perception that they need to encompass some now not possible fantastic that lets in you to get hold of love.

Others can assist this boom through way of: Providing a manual system to deal with intervals of sadness, spotting that intimacy may be a trigger of feelings of loss.

Famous Romantics encompass many Writers, Musicians, Artists and Actors:

Jackie Kennedy Onassis, Frédéric Chopin, Annie Lennox, Yukio Mishima, Pyotr I. Tchaikovsky, Lars von Trier, Marlon Brando, Anne Frank, Edgar Allen Poe, Cindy Sherman, Virginia Woolf, Karen Blixen / Isak Dinesen, Anaîs Nin, Miles Davis, Hank Williams, Frida Kahlo, Leonard Cohen, Billie

Holiday, Maria Callas, Keith Jarrett, Cher, Stevie Nicks, Bob Dylan, Paul Simon, Tennessee Williams, J.D. Salinger, Sarah McLachlan, Alanis Morrissette, Amy Winehouse, Ingmar Bergman, Martha Graham, Angelina Jolie, Gustav Mahler, Jeremy Irons, Winona Ryder, Kate Winslet, Joni Mitchell, Nicolas Cage, and Johnny Depp.

Related Types

Every persona kind is inspired with the aid of the wings to the thing that they may mixture into surely definitely certainly one of them. If a character type has a robust wing, it will make a large effect at the person's persona.

Performer 3 (wing): When a Romantic has an inclination towards the Performer wing, they'll be extra extroverted and notable, even turning into flamboyant and bold. The Romantic and the Performer are even more cautiously associated than distinctive related sorts because of the reality they percent the equal Heart Center kinds. They each are passionate about getting specific human beings's approval and reputation. Their extreme creativity lets in them in their artwork, however they every may be aggressive. Their variations are that Performers are usually targeted on a future goal, on the same time as Romantics are heaps a lot much less so, for the reason that they're frequently distracted thru using their inner recognition.

Observer five (wing): When a Romantic has a bent toward the Observer wing, they turn out to be greater introverted and highbrow. They can usually have a tendency inside the course of idiosyncratic conduct and are much more likely to be depressed. These sorts percent an analytical, introspective nature, but the distinction is that Romantics are the maximum emotional kind, whilst the Observers stay greater detached and have more defined personal boundaries.

Security Type: Perfectionist 1: When the Romantic is shifting towards the safety type, Perfectionist 1, they may surrender their green with envy and emotionally turbulent dispositions to turn out to be extra goal and principled, sharing the great functions of healthful Perfectionists.

Stress Type: Giver 2: When the Romantic is transferring towards the pressure type, the Romantic becomes emotionally clingy and overly concerned, just like the worst traits of the Giver.

Overlaps Between the Romantic and Other Non-associated Types

Perfectionist 1: These sorts are carefully associated because of the fact the Perfectionist is the safety shape of the Romantic and the Romantic is the stress form of the Perfectionist. These sorts are both very expressive in their beliefs, and that they show an unflagging willpower to enhancing themselves. However, the

Perfectionist is specific due to the reality his or her idealism is all focused on "getting it proper" however the Romantic is pushed thru obtaining non-public fulfilment. Another massive difference has to do with the reality that Perfectionists are repressed, at the same time as Romantics may be self-absorbed to the element of drowning in their emotions.

Loyal Skeptic 6: The shared tendencies between the Romantic and the Loyal Skeptic are that every sorts can oppose authority, even to the component of recklessly brushing off the regulations and concerning themselves in risky conditions. The sorts moreover percentage times of self-doubt and thinking. However, the principle distinction is that Loyal Skeptics genuinely do now not need to be wrapped up indefinitely in feelings of longing or choice, at the identical time as Romantics do. The special huge difference is that Romantics are searching for the element they revel in they'll be missing, while the Loyal Skeptic is more often trying to find what may also circulate incorrect an excellent manner to decorate it.

Epicure 7: These sorts are regularly considered appearance-alikes because of their comparable intensity, idealism and preference for adventure and stimulation. Both types are deeply devoted to living a lifestyles via their acute emotional faculties. The largest distinction comes in phrases in their mood. Epicures are active, fantastic and powerful. They searching out pride and avoid ache. Romantics are the opposite, as they're characterised with the useful resource of melancholic emotions.

Mediator 9: The Romantic and the Mediator are taken into consideration to be look alike kinds because of their shared orientation towards relationships. Both sorts are loving, nurturing and feature a high degree of empathy. At the equal time, every kinds can get deeply immersed of their surroundings, to the factor of feeling misplaced or disoriented. Both sorts additionally risk despair growing from their steady need to self-deprecate. The biggest difference amongst Mediators and Romantics is available in terms of their courting to others. While the Romantic is directed inwards and relishes the sensation of being particular and unique, the Mediator is all about mixing in with the institution that lets in you to avoid warfare.

Chapter 5: The Observer

Type Five is the Observer, the sort that most wants to check out why things are the manner they're. They need to recognize every little detail how the entire global works with a hobby that encompasses every aspect the natural international further to the inner geographical areas in their imaginations. They are the folks which can be continually looking, asking proving questions, and delving deeply into matters. The Observer does now not just take delivery of obtained attention and dogma. Instead, they experience a burning want to check the reality of maximum assumptions for themselves. For this purpose, some of the splendid inventors in data may be considered Observers.

One of the paradoxes of the Observer type is that however the truth that they are generally searching out knowledge—and generally finding it—they preserve to anticipate that they may be no longer correct sufficient to feature successfully in a few component location they discover themselves. Their worst misperception approximately themselves is they do not have an ability to do subjects in addition to others. In order to catch up on this, they do not attempt to interact right away with sports activities sports and people that is probably capable of supply their self notion a miles-wished leg up. Instead, the common tactic for the Observer is to triumph over a retreat returned into the specifically advanced global in their minds wherein they're capable of experience greater succesful. They cling to the conviction that outstanding from the protection of their will they in the end be capable of parent out the manner to do everything. Although they inform themselves that, in some unspecified time within the future, they plan to rejoin the world, at the prevailing time will in no way come, except the Observer is capable of locate stability.

The Observer, just like the numerous differing types, may be quite numerous. Although they surely spend numerous time gazing and thinking about, the point of interest of their immoderate hobby can be massive or small, natural or made thru humans, ostentatious or diffused. Whatever observations they pick out out to make, their unconscious act of immersing in them as deeply as feasible is what allows them to begin to internalize their knowledge and slowly collect a experience of self-self assurance. After reflecting deeply on some given hassle, they then enjoy able to going out into public (however small) and sharing what they recognize. They will never virtually rush into a few new hobby or soar out of their seats to speak at a assembly. This reflective outstanding way they will be well poised to find out thrilling new facts or make new contemporary mixtures based mostly on what they have determined; the healthy Observers truly do now not in reality spit returned out the information, like a machine. The possibility to share what they apprehend is extraordinarily crucial to their psyche because of the truth wonderful after they get verification in their tough-earned observations and thoroughly crafted hypotheses, or see that others apprehend their artwork, do they revel in that their competency has been showed. This fulfills their primary desire to be knowledgeable that they recognize what they're speakme approximately.

The most important capabilities for the Observer are intelligence, information, and belief due to the fact their whole experience of self is constructed round having thoughts. To the amount that the texture unique, it is due to the fact they consider they'll be someone who has a few factor unique and insightful to make a contribution to the company. Because of this cause, the Observer isn't always the handiest who can be inclined to tread a well-worn course. If it is already familiar and nicely-set up, neglect approximately it. Instead, the test comes alive at the same time as their hobby is interested by the unknown, the subjects the common character overlooks, the deep secrets and techniques and techniques and strategies—even to the thing of intense enchantment to conspiracies, to the occult, to the extraordinary, and to the unthinkable. To excite an Observer, inform them, it has in no manner been executed in advance than – and it could in no way be done. When the Observer is invited to research unknown territory, the incentive of understanding a few component that others do not understand or growing some factor that no individual has ever professional will supply them a totally precise location that no man or woman else occupies. For them, cultivating this niche is the excellent manner for them to try and gather the ones elusive characteristics of independence and of self warranty.

For this motive, it is critical for the Observer to maintain a revel in of safety and well-being by way of attaching themselves to a exquisite vicinity wherein they're an expert. This will they allow them to experience confident and related with the arena round them. The Observer will have a tendency to count on that it is vital to first learn how to do some aspect definitely well, and then they will be able to meet the worrying situations of lifestyles. As they do that, but, they enjoy an severe annoyance towards, or perhaps an aggression, towards every exceptional matters that distract them or get of their manner, whether or not or not or not they are their loved ones or outdoor limitations. Because of this excessive electricity, they focus unyieldingly to a few issue they experience they will draw near and revel in regular approximately, whether or not or no longer it's miles an intellectual, ingenious or bodily pursuit. Just due to the fact someone is an Observer, that does not advocate they're a scholar or perhaps thrive in an academic surroundings. Depending on their social occasions and their intelligence, they focus intensely on studying a few thing that has captured their hobby. It does now not want to be some thing a brilliant manner to constantly rocket them to popularity and wealth. It can be, but it is able to additionally be studying a way to restoration a vehicle or becoming the quality scuba diver within the international.

Observers typically will be predisposed to explore regions that don't situation what their buddies or own family remember them, whether or now not for better or worse. In truth, they do not find it impossible to resist at the equal time as remarkable humans take shipping of as proper with their thoughts too fast because it makes them begin to worry that their thoughts is probably too stupid and no longer specific sufficient. It follows, then, that information is whole of well-known Observers who went closer to traditional strategies of wondering or doing topics (which incorporates the scientist Darwin, the physicist Einstein, and the truth seeker Nietzsche). These are the a fulfillment Observers. Many greater, however, usually have a tendency to turn out to be misplaced within the opaque complexities of their tangled mental techniques. The result is they can turn out to be eccentric, socially remoted folks who contribute little to society – a brilliant waste in their large capability.

The way in which Observers can intensely pay interest is liable for first-rate discoveries and global changing enhancements at the same time as they are healthful and fluid of their personalities. However, at the same time as the Observer's man or woman is extra obsessive, it may moreover with out difficulty paintings to growth self-defeating challenges that emerge as insurmountable boundaries. This is due to the fact they become getting distracted from the important realistic problems that want attention, precisely due to the truth that their interest is targeted some place else. Regardless of no matter the assets of their anxieties might be—whether or no longer they revel in they may be vulnerable in phrases of interpersonal relationships, or bodily energy, or capacity to find significant work—not unusual Observers prefer to keep away from having to address the ones critical lifestyles questions. Instead, they push it off via discovering a few aspect else to attention on on the manner to purpose them to experience greater successful. However, regardless of what degree of mastery they'll be capable of cultivate of their decided on location of statistics, they're plagued with a terrible end end result: this expertise is in no way enough in curing their essential insecurities about how they characteristic inside the global. For example, as an astrologist, a Five also can need to observe the entirety there can be to apprehend about horoscopes, however if the worry is that they will be never going which will run a marathon fast enough, they may no longer have solved their critical worry that their have a look at have become trying to mask.

One of the most complex regions to dealing without delay with are bodily topics, as Observers enjoy specifically put off by way of using the risk of having to get their arms truely grimy. For this cause, they spend a tremendous deal in their waking hours on amassing information and developing mind and abilities that they actually acquire as actual with will lead them to experience prepared to face anything undertaking should possibly face them. They are desperately worried with maintaining the entirety that they have ever studied; their reason is in case you need to bring it spherical in their heads, and so as that they have an inclination to disdain folks who rely on "artificial" aids, which includes net generation. This creates similarly struggling for the Observer because at some point of the time in which they may be engaged on this extended approach, they do no longer want to engage meaningfully with one-of-a-kind human beings. This effects in a in addition decrease in lots of exceptional sensible and social capabilities, which places them similarly out of stability. Then they begin a vicious cycle wherein they experience a want to spend increasingly more time gathering and analyzing the effects in their efforts, or maybe less to any hobby that might be associated with what they really need.

Therefore, the venture that is going via all but the maximum balanced of the Observers is to try to apprehend that they will be capable of pursue each single one of the questions or issues that may spark their imaginations, but on the same time, it's far feasible for them to keep their relationships, take top care of themselves, and participate in all of the behavior which might be the bedrock of a healthy lifestyles.

The related styles of the observer are:

Wing: Romantic four

Wing: Loyal Skeptic 6

Security Type: Protector 8

Stress Type: Epicure 7

The maximum commonplace appearance-alike non-related forms of the Observer are:

Perfectionist 1

The possibility of kinds (differing types to keep in thoughts if Observer is your top end result):

65% Observer five

eleven% Loyal Skeptic 6

eleven% Mediator 9

Based on those opportunities, if you scored high at the Observer check, there is a 65% chance it's far your correct kind. However, there may be additionally an 11% threat of you being a Loyal Skeptic or a Mediator. If you scored immoderate on the ones checks as nicely, look at the distinguishing sections under cautiously to peer if those could definitely be your type. Remember, if a first-class kind has a sturdy wing of one or the alternative, which could considerably have an impact on how the character manifests itself. If you can't get hold of the type you are, your feelings can be valid, or may be a give up end result of the bad stereotypes you've got heard about the kind, so ensure to discover any strong reactions you can have.

Myths About the Observer

One of the maximum powerfully horrible myths about the Observer is that they may be grasping, selfish and avaricious, even as in fact they will be very giving and engaged—so long as they revel in that there are clean barriers installing how masses they are predicted to present.

Adjectives Describing the Observer

Thoughtful, indifferent, objective, analytic, informed, smart, intellectual, unassuming, are the high quality capabilities. Miserly, unfeeling, withholding, indifferent, passive, distant, some distance flung, are the bad capabilities.

The Underlying Truths of the Observer

The easy principle the Observer has forgotten: There is sufficient know-how gift within the natural order to fulfill each person dreams.

The Observer wrongly believes: The worldwide is attacking me; I want to retreat as a manner to nourish myself. If I supply my full self, I will be depleted and faded.

The Observer created those behaviors to compensate: Because of the perception that the whole lot is a call for at the Observer, they usually have a tendency to try to defend themselves with the aid of the use of trying a good deal much less and nourishing myself with knowledge as an possibility.

The Characteristics that Define the Observer

Because of these adaptive behaviors, the Observer generally makes a speciality of: All matters intellectual and intention, alongside aspect facts and figures, and statistics. The Observer could be very sensitive about any functionality intrusions onto his or her time. They usually have problem trusting a enjoy of abundance and hundreds, which ends up in self-deprivation and rejecting the offer for manual from others.

They placed their energy into: Keeping themselves at a distance from the ones round them, together with cherished ones, in case you want to be in a better function to look at. They are best satisfied inside the event that they feel they apprehend the entirety approximately a given problem. They can quality embark on a modern undertaking in the event that they revel in sincerely prepared in advance. They additionally placed sizable strive into blocking their emotions as definitely as feasible. They experience this is the exceptional manner to hold their energy. They are the fantastic kind at retaining barriers and limits with others, and they jealously shield their privacy. These trends, even as the Observer is out of stability, can with out hassle emerge as the extremely good impediment to his or her happiness.

They desperately try to keep away from: Intense emotions in absolutely everyone and absolutely everyone, cherished ones and co-people, or perhaps themselves. Their least favourite feeling is worry, which makes them pretty threat adverse. They experience threatened through way of humans or subjects which is probably demanding in their time. These humans are doubly unsightly to the Observer because of the truth they have a tendency to make him sense inadequate, this is each different feeling the Observer is primed to study. This excessive distance that the lousy Observer takes from everyone will regularly bring about a revel in of emptiness, which the Observer fills via gaining knowledge of and reading extra.

They have those strengths: Academics. Intellectual endeavors. Possessing facts. Being thoughtful. Keeping calm in a scenario of catastrophe. Being sincere and reliable. Appreciating crucial subjects in lifestyles.

They communicate inside the following manner: They commonly have a propensity to hold their recognition on the statistics of the trouble, in region of on making an difficult verbal exchange fashion. They can be genuine, clean and properly spoken, but human beings might likely understand this as being far flung and aloof, or perhaps terse and disinterested.

The Sources of Stress, Anger and Defensiveness

They are pressured by the usage of way of: Any incursions into their non-public existence, boundaries or obstacles. They get unduly pressured out even as they're feeling tired and spent, more than one of a kind character types inside the enneagram. They bristle in opposition to the possibility of trying some issue from someone that could engender a dependence. They reject sturdy emotion. The responsibility to analyze each component of a problem in advance than taking motion simply reasons pressure in an unstable Observer, even though it will seem that they will be taking up the research willingly.

They are angered approximately: When a person thinks the observer is incorrect, they may be capable of frequently fly into an surprising mood. Not having sufficient time to regenerate and repair themselves.

They are protecting within the path of: People who make desires on their time; the observer hates surprising knocks at the door, or maybe surprise mobile smartphone calls.

Their anger and defensiveness are characterized as such: Angry outbursts that come unexpectedly. Withdrawn conduct that now and again may be careworn with their everyday have a take a look at behavior – that is normally intentional, and serves as a further protection mechanism, so that the observer is able to deny the fact that he is having emotions.

Personal Growth

Their final intention is: To apprehend that there may be abundance in life an top notch way to simply renew itself, imparting the Observer what he or she goals in the end of her journey.

They can in addition this boom through: Observing once they withhold thoughts and emotions, spotting that wondering can update feeling, questioning the avoidance of emotions, locating strategies to unite frame, coronary coronary heart and thoughts. Expressing their emotions in a strong place. Learning to talk brazenly with others and display secrets and techniques and strategies without fear of turning into based definitely. Not usually being an count on.

Their largest obstacle is: Keeping all non-public facts close to their chest, questioning they could remedy everything with common sense, now not truly connecting with the humans they love, withholding their time and power for fear of being depleted with the aid of the adverse global.

Others can guide this increase with the aid of: Helping them query the three lethal S's: secrecy, superiority and separateness, encouraging spontaneity and indicates of emotion, presenting them a safe location wherein to reveal emotion, allowing them to apprehend they may be seen—and that it hurts when they withdraw. Not traumatic that they generally have the answers and celebrating as soon as they interact in some new employer with out overly getting ready themselves. Giving comments after they explicit themselves, however with some restraint at the beginning just so it isn't overwhelming.

Practical recommendations for the Observer:

•Take extra risks.

•Try throwing a big, spontaneous collecting.

•Speak up with out reading excessively.

•Try sports activities or inventive sports in new areas.

•Ground yourself within the gift.

•Get a massage to feel greater decided in your body.

•Go to treatment to exercising being more communicative about private troubles.

Famous Observers

(Because Observers aren't regularly public figures, quite a few the ones are a lot plenty less extensively recognized "well-known" humans, in assessment to exclusive types which might be greater extroverted and, because of this, get delight from media attention. They encompass severa geniuses, entrepreneurs and artists):

Siddartha Gautama Buddha, Vincent van Gogh, Albert Einstein, Friedrich Nietzsche, Georgia O'Keefe, Stephen Hawking, Oliver Sacks, John Nash (A Beautiful Mind), Edvard Munch, Salvador Dali, Werner Herzog, Bill Gates, Agatha Christie, Susan Sontag, Alfred Hitchcock, Laurie Anderson, Emily Dickinson, James Joyce, Stephen King, Ursula K. LeGuin, Eckhart Tolle, Meredith Monk, Clive Barker, David Byrne, Mark Zuckerberg, A.H. Almaas, Glenn Gould, John

Cage, Jodie Foster, Kurt Cobain, Marlene Dietrich, Peter Gabriel, Trent Reznor, Thom York (Radiohead), David Lynch, Stanley Kubrick, David Cronenberg, Tim Burton, David Fincher, "The Far Side" Gary Larson, Jane Goodall, and "Wikileaks" Julian Assange.

Related Types

Every personality kind is added approximately thru the wings to the problem that they may mixture into considered one in all them. If a person kind has a sturdy wing, it'll make a big effect on the character's person.

Romantic 4 (wing): If the Observer has a strong 4 wing, they may be extra progressive and empathetic and lots a good deal less robotic and analytical. They could have a tendency to self-absorbed, however.

Loyal Skeptic 6 (wing): If the Observer has a robust six wing, they'll be extra dependable, but they will additionally suffer extra from an extra of warning and additionally a revel in of hysteria. These Observers will gravitate inside the direction of STEM fields.

Protector eight (security type): When the Observer moves closer to the fantastic facet of their safety kind, they'll have an less complicated time moving into contact with all elements of their body, thoughts and soul. They should have a keener take transport of as real with in their instincts and revel in more confident asserting themselves even though they revel in challenged. When angered, they may have a extra enough experience of strength in preference to feeling depleted. They may be effective at setting limitations and limits.

When the Observer movements within the route of the terrible aspect of their safety type, they'll lose touch with common feel and lash out in anger. They may be extra up the front about their refusal to widely known human beings's emotions and requests, and they will also be openly damaging and without a trouble attack folks that call for matters of them.

Epicure 7 (strain kind): When the Observer movements in the direction of the notable aspect in their stress kind, they will be more open to existence research, be greater snug in their very very very own pores and pores and skin and less awkward, be open to attempting new memories and are looking for for fun and adventure.

When the Observer movements in the direction of the horrible component in their pressure kind, they will be distracted and impulsive, even reckless in their choice of duties and sports. This kind of behavior can precipitate a catastrophe, at the way to ultimately be a comfort to the Observer who's unable to discover a few other manner to explicit their suffering.

Overlaps Between the Observer and Other Non-related Types

Perfectionist 1: Perfectionists and Observers are look-alikes due to their shared willpower to highbrow agency and their tendency to withdraw into themselves whilst they will be jogging out some type of hassle. Their primary difference is that at the same time as Perfectionists are immoderate, Observers artwork to maintain their power. They are content material cloth to stay and allow stay at the same time as the Perfectionist constantly strives for their personal development—and for the improvement of others. They cannot allow properly sufficient on my own.

Loyal Skeptic 6: The Observer and the Loyal Skeptic effects aggregate into every other particularly due to the fact they are wings and each part of the Head Center. They proportion numerous man or woman traits such as a bent within the path of analytical wondering. They are extra thinkers than doers, and face up to taking motion till in reality organized. Their versions are that

Observers paintings to detach themselves from their emotions to the element of numbness. They are masters at compartmentalization. Loyal Skeptics, as an alternative, are more reactive. They will be predisposed to be greater immoderate and can exaggerate the danger to which they are exposed. They can't detach themselves from their environment, no longer just like the Observer who excels at this.

Mediator 9: The Mediator and the Observer can be taken into consideration to be appearance alike kinds due to the fact they every may be introverted and withdrawn, considerate and reflective. Both kinds can fade into the data and keep away from being inspired via way of way in their environment. Their foremost difference comes from the reality that the Observer is keen to detach themselves from their cherished ones in order to protect their fragile experience of personal place and to say their independence. Mediators, at the opposite, are the sort which are maximum quite definitely associated with superb humans to the point that they combination in with them with the reason of maintaining all matters non violent and calm.

Chapter 6: The Loyal Skeptic

Personality type six, the Loyal Skeptic, is of all of the persona sorts, the maximum unswerving to their friends in addition to to their non-public beliefs. The Loyal Skeptic is the type so as to be most probably to head down with the sinking ship. This obviously has a immoderate top notch connotation, but additionally a lousy one, due to the reality that they are inclined to dangle directly to soured relationships of all kinds for a good buy longer than all of the one among a kind character sorts. This belief of loyalty furthermore extends past humans and holds for thoughts, systems, and beliefs. This does now not propose that they will be blindly reliable considering they will be frequently dependable to the willpower of questioning anyone's thoughts. In the maximum extreme of times, a Loyal Skeptic might also have a suspicious kind of thoughts-set, firmly defensive the notion that government in desired must be at a loss for words or perhaps outright defied. Loyalty on this persona type does now not equate with usually (or ever) getting into conjunction with the "reputation quo." In fact, their requirements is probably defiantly rebellious and anti-authoritarian to the factor of being brazenly innovative. Regardless of what the Loyal Skeptic's beliefs actually are, they will will be predisposed to fight for them with more intensity than they certainly try and fight for themselves, even though it subsequently finally ends up hurting them. They can even shield their community, family or social organisation with the equal intensity— regardless of how steep the price.

To recognize why the Loyal Skeptic is so unflaggingly reliable to others, it's far crucial to apprehend their easy fear: that they do now not want to be deserted and abandoned with no person to beneficial aid them. For this reason, the precept trouble for the Loyal Skeptic is a catastrophe of their self-self belief. The Loyal Skeptic includes anticipate that they're lacking any of the internal belongings needed to cope with existence's problems on their very non-public. For this reason, they flip to something outdoor guide in order to live on. This can also moreover need to include bureaucratic or institutional structures, political allies, or maybe personal ideals. If they can't discover gift systems which may be appropriate to their desires, they'll move to date as to create their very very own and dedicate big interest to supporting them thrive.

Since the Loyal Skeptic is the primary type of the Head Center, it way that they have the most hassle tapping into their non-public internal guidance. Because of this issue, they typically lack self assurance in their private mind, judgments and opinions, even though they have got studied the problem carefully.

This problem does not suggest that the Loyal Skeptic does not use commonplace sense and reason. Actually, it's far quite the other. They expect continuously to the problem that they typically tend towards anxiety and neurosis. Because of this, they prevaricate whilst it comes time to make critical life alternatives as they can get caught in a loop of fear. At the equal time, they are no longer the sort in order to bypass taking walks to others to have them make picks on their behalf. While they deeply need to avoid being managed, they may be caught by their worry of taking duty in this kind of way that might positioned them on the ultra-modern seat and like, as an alternative, to fly under the radar or to keep a low profile.

For better or for worse, the Loyal Skeptic thinks so much that they're painfully aware about their anxieties. They often search for approaches to try and make protection strategies in opposition to these dispositions. This can be a supply of electricity and luxury, an effective crutch, due to the truth if the Loyal Skeptic feels that they have got sufficient all over again up (whether or now not via their personal help community or, for the greater isolated kind sixes, thru a device of ideals), then they revel in capable of bypass in advance with their plans with a few diploma of self guarantee. But if the manual is missing or feeble, they quickly spiral downwards of their emotions of hysteria and self-doubt causing their number one fear to rear its unpleasant head and knock them once more a few paces. The Loyal Skeptic desires to impeach their burning want for safety, frequently asking themselves what safety is and the manner do they understand if it's miles sufficient. In the absence of touch with their intuitive inner steering and the profound feeling of help that it confers, the Loyal Skeptic is in a in no way-completing warfare to discover their footing and launch themselves earlier in life.

Because of their want for beneficial resource, the Loyal Skeptic is often on a undertaking boom a nexus of receive as genuine with atop this undercurrent of anxiety and uncertainty. When they come upon this feeling of tension, they can not decide out why they feel it, which then makes them contemplate similarly reasons at the back of it – in the absence of cause, the Loyal Skeptic will simply make some thing up. Because they may be so tenacious of their ideals, whilst the Loyal Skeptic invents a reason for their anxiety, it is going to be very tough to dissuade them of that justification, so it's miles higher to save you them from starting first of all. Since they are desperate to experience that there is some element concrete and clear of their lives, they effortlessly end up overly connected to justifications or worldwide perspectives that appear to provide an explanation for their ache. Since the Loyal Skeptic faces trouble in obtaining a assured enjoy of "perception" (therefore, skeptic) and due to the truth it is so crucial to their feeling of well-being, when they undertake a honest belief, they do no longer like to impeach it, nor do they want others to carry out that (due to this, dependable). This is also actual for people inside the life of the Loyal Skeptic. Once the Loyal Skeptic feels they are able to count on a person, they may be joined at the hip with that character, going to remarkable (even excessive) lengths to hold and red meat up connections with the individual that acts as their sounding board. This could be a trainer, a mentor, or in reality a chum who's capable of temper the emotional reactions and conduct of the Loyal Skeptic. Here is some specific area wherein their loyalty shines through, as they will necessarily do the entirety and something of their strength to preserve their relationships afloat. This character becomes a surrogate for their personal internal guidance, and they make bigger to them the consider they can not extend to themselves.

Because of this probably horrible dynamic, the Loyal Skeptic who isn't in touch with their private internal steering bounces back and forth among anything competing influences is probably swatting them toughest at a wonderful second in time. Since the Loyal Skeptic is so reactive, it manner that it's far hard to constantly keep them inside a given definition. It seems as in spite of the fact that something that is probably stated about the Loyal Skeptic also can be actual inside the contrary. Thus, the Loyal Skeptic is frequently sides of the identical coin with all of the contradictions in whole show. They may be competitive and passive, concerned and courageous, terrific and impolite, powerful and prone, trusting and diffident, defenders and aggressors, bullies and sufferers, fans and leaders, extroverted and introverted, sensitive and silly, beneficiant and stingy, magnanimous and petty, cooperative and unhelpful, thinkers and doers, the list is going on and on. This contradiction is the primary calling card of the Loyal Skeptic as they lack a connection to their inner steerage and grow to be turning into contradiction personified—to their frustration and the frustration of their circle of relatives and co-personnel.

As they search for a steady environment without trying to find to get a manage on their emotional anxiety, the Loyal Skeptic is the author in their personal worst issues. Fortunately, after they do discover ways to treatment their emotional insecurities, however, the Loyal Skeptic is acquainted with that regardless of the fact that the arena is continuously evolving and is, via definition, unsure, they may be able to appearance inside themselves to discover their personal serenity and braveness in the hardest of conditions. With this little however profound shift, the Loyal Skeptic might be able to get admission to and proliferate the maximum essential present of all, that is having an internal revel in of peace regardless of how loopy the arena can be.

The associated sorts of the Loyal Skeptic are:

Wing: Observer five

Wing: Epicure 7

Security Type: Mediator 9

Stress Type: Performer 3

Most commonplace look-alike types:

Romantic 4

Protector 8

The possibility of kinds (other kinds to undergo in mind if Loyal Skeptic is your pinnacle desire):

Based on the ones opportunities, if you scored immoderate on the Loyal Skeptic check, there may be a 66% threat it's far your accurate type. However, there may be additionally an 8% chance of you being an Observer or a Mediator, and a 5% risk of being both a Romantic or an Epicure. If you scored excessive on those exams as properly, take a look at the distinguishing sections under cautiously to look if those have to genuinely be your kind. Remember, if a positive kind has a strong wing of 1 or the possibility, that could significantly influence how the man or woman manifests itself. If you can not get keep of the kind you are, your emotions can be legitimate, or may be a cease end result of the lousy stereotypes you have got were given heard approximately the sort, so ensure to discover any strong reactions you could have.

Myths approximately the Loyal Skeptic

The worst myths approximately the Loyal Skeptic are that they're pessimistic and diffident. They can appear overly timid. However, the Loyal Skeptic questions topics with a motive of improving their existence. When someone earns their obtain as proper with, they may be extremely trusting—they honestly take longer to open up to humans than the commonplace wholesome individual.

Adjectives Describing the Loyal Skeptic

On the brilliant trouble, dependable, annoying, collaborative, analytical, informed, responsible, dependable, honest, high-quality. On the horrific side, mistrustful, skeptical, worrying overly vigilant and asks too many questions.

The Underlying Truths of the Loyal Skeptic

The clean principle the Loyal Skeptic has forgotten: At the straight away of our transport, people are all endowed with a sense of consider in ourselves and in our universe.

The Loyal Skeptic wrongly believes: That the arena is a threatening location and, therefore, all authority shouldn't be depended on.

The Loyal Skeptic created those behaviors to compensate: There are first-rate processes a Loyal Skeptic can appear, that may create further confusion approximately the type, as they will be pretty unique. The accommodating stance of the Loyal Skeptic manner that they'll have a tendency to just accept authority after thinking it if you want to avoid functionality threats. The difficult stance of the Loyal Skeptic method that they will hold to battle authority because the perceived way to keep protecting themselves from any perceived hazard.

The Characteristics that Define the Loyal Skeptic

Because of those adaptive behaviors, the Loyal Skeptic makes a speciality of: Anything that might move incorrect, the worst-case state of affairs, feasible threats and dangers, and hidden implications. The Loyal Skeptic does now not genuinely take a look at the ones threats however magnifies them.

The Loyal Skeptic places their electricity into: Challenging humans, analyzing conditions, checking out, decoding, looking for capability assets of safety in robust humans, keeping loyalties and fighting for a well worth cause.

The Loyal Skeptic desperately tries to keep away from: Feeling based completely without any functionality to control a unstable scenario. Being helpless. Losing treasured relationships. Facing hazard.

The Loyal Skeptic has those strengths: Fortitude, dependability, intuitive nature, applicable sense of humor, kindness, experience of duty, interrogative attitude, protecting, warmth and constant.

The Loyal Skeptic communicates within the following way: It generally has a tendency inside the direction of an excessive, whether or not or no longer it's far overly drawn out or fast fire. Regardless, they are continuously asking questions, and this will be perceived as a energy or susceptible element relying at the thoughts-set of the person managing all the questions.

The Sources of Stress, Anger and Defensiveness for the Loyal Skeptic

The Loyal Skeptic is pressured via: The ordinary feeling of stress whilst they are attempting to resolve the way to deal with topics they can't absolutely recognize. Any hassle with an professional determine. The threat of losing critical alliances.

The Loyal Skeptic is angered about: Betrayal and deception, feeling trapped, having immoderate desires positioned on their time and susceptible authority figures.

The Loyal Skeptic is protecting toward: People who forget about them.

Their anger and defensiveness are characterized as such: In the wonderful case, it comes off as funny, in the worst case it reads as sarcastic or perhaps outright competitive.

Personal Growth

Their final reason is: To be capable of recollect in him or herself, and in different human beings, pushing doubt and mistrust out in their minds.

They can further this boom with the useful resource of: Insisting on smooth guidelines in collaboration, proscribing procrastination through committing to timelines, weighing exquisite and horrible further and checking in with their fight or flight instincts.

Their largest impediment is: Knowing how to be their very very own deliver of internal steerage. Refusing to save you being busy all of the time as a defense mechanism. Dwelling at the worst-case scenario. Insisting on obtaining actuality earlier than persevering with on with dwelling their lives.

Others can help this boom thru the usage of: Providing a reality test with the aid of asking them to call their fears out loud, heading off moving into doubtful agreements, imparting a reliable help tool and usually being reliable.

Practical Suggestions for The Loyal Skeptic:

•Develop self perception thru surrounding your self with excellent individuals who will encourage you.

•Make a intellectual study (or even a bodily one) of incredible compliments you get preserve of.

•Keep an open thoughts approximately distinct lifestyles.

•When you are making a mistake, tell your self it is good sufficient.

•Try to snort at your self.

•Consider breaking down your largest responsibilities into plausible segments.

•Practice patience with others.

•Try meditation or respiration bodily games.

•Give yourself permission to loosen up with out feeling responsible.

•Try a state-of-the-art bodily hobby, even supposing it is without a doubt as clean as taking a each day stroll.

Related Types

Every character kind is recommended with the aid of the wings to the element that they may combination into really absolutely considered one of them. If a man or woman kind has a strong wing, it's going to make a huge effect at the character's persona.

The Observer five (wing): The Observer and the Loyal Skeptic without problems aggregate into each other in particular because they're wings and every a part of the Head Center. They percent severa character traits which embody a bent in the direction of analytical wondering. They are more thinkers than doers, and face up to taking movement until simply prepared. Their variations are that Observers paintings to detach themselves from their emotions to the issue of numbness. They are masters at compartmentalization. Loyal Skeptics, as an alternative, are more reactive. They will be predisposed to be greater extreme and can exaggerate the danger to which they'll be uncovered. They cannot detach themselves from their surroundings, in contrast to the Observer who excels at this. The Loyal Skeptic with a extra advanced Observer wing will become more highbrow and offers off remote thoughts-set. They can be the most introverted of the sixes, and will also be inclined to be extra tentative.

Epicure 7 (wing): The Loyal Skeptic with a extra advanced Epicure wing might be extroverted. Rather than pursuing intellectual dreams, they will lean within the route of materialism and is probably extra apt in a career rather than academia. They also may be greater active to the thing of turning into impulsive.

Mediator nine (protection kind): These types have plenty in commonplace as they're reciprocally associated. Not best is the mediator the safety shape of the Loyal Skeptic, the Loyal Skeptic is the strain kind of the Mediator. When the Loyal Skeptic is greater accommodating, they percentage traits with the Mediator insofar as they each are exceptional and eager to satisfaction. They may be touchy, easy to genuinely take delivery of something in reality everybody tells them to do, and determined to avoid conflict. Secure Loyal Skeptics are capable of take shipping of existence for what it is. Stressed Mediators emerge as greater stressful and ready to jump into movement. The maximum essential distinction is that Loyal Skeptics have a tendency to keep distance among themselves and others, at the identical time as Mediators threat being sincerely absorbed into the requests and personalities of these they love. Mediators without hassle agree with whomever, at the equal time as Loyal Skeptics will check out all the viable results of a certain path of movement.

When the Loyal Skeptic is capable of pass within the route of the high-quality thing of their safety type, they're greater superior of their functionality to empathize with exquisite human beings. They are a whole lot much less narrow of their information of the arena. They are more likely a wonderful manner to chortle at themselves and receive as authentic with their inner guidance.

When the Loyal Skeptic is forced to transport towards the terrible facet in their safety type, they are able to actually chance falling right right into a drug dependency or melancholy. They might possibly appear like honestly disconnected from truth and missing any hobby in some thing.

Performer three (pressure kind): These sorts are associated because of the reality the Performer is the pressure shape of the Loyal Skeptic and the Loyal Skeptic is the safety form of the Performer. Both sorts proportion a pleasing, humans stunning individual. Although, Performers have a propensity to be greater strong and trusting once they go with the waft closer to sixes, on the same time as Loyal Skeptics in stress end up greater active and keen to meet their dreams. When the Loyal Skeptic is capable of pass closer to the nice aspect of their strain type, they'll be capable of make alternatives extra correctly and take awesome moves. They can understand all their accomplishments. When the Loyal Skeptic is compelled to move within the route of the terrible side in their pressure kind, they preserve themselves so busy they turn out to be workaholics, in no way try something new if there may be any hazard at all, undertake fake identities to keep themselves stable or even resort to mendacity.

Overlaps Between the Loyal Skeptic and Other Non-associated Types

Romantic 4: The shared developments among the Loyal Skeptic and the Romantic are that both types can oppose authority even to the factor of recklessly disregarding the hints and related to themselves in volatile conditions. These sorts moreover percentage instances of doubting themselves to the component of paralysis. However, the main difference is that Romantics truly need to be wrapped up indefinitely in feelings of longing or choice, even as Loyal Skeptics do not. The different large distinction is that the Loyal Skeptic is greater often attempting to find what might probable bypass incorrect at the manner to decorate it on the identical time as Romantics are attempting to find the issue, they revel in is lacking.

Loyal Skeptic 6: The shared developments among the Romantic and the Loyal Skeptic are that each sorts can oppose authority even to the issue of recklessly brushing off the policies and associated with themselves in unstable situations. These sorts additionally share instances of self-doubt. However, the primary difference is that Loyal Skeptics simply do no longer want to be wrapped up indefinitely in emotions of longing or choice at the equal time as Romantics do. The awesome big distinction is that Romantics are in search of the issue they feel they may be missing on the same time because the Loyal Skeptic is more frequently on the lookout for what may additionally flow into wrong if you need to decorate it.

The Protector 8: The Protector and Loyal Skeptics who take a hard stance have plenty in common. They have the tendency in the direction of aggression and provocative, confrontational conduct when they deem a purpose definitely well worth to combat for. They every will be predisposed to be untrusting inside the course of the arena. When they spring into motion, however, we will see their vital versions. Loyal Skeptics will will be predisposed to be more reflective as they count on out the worst-case scenario for their actions, which might also halt them in their tracks. Protectors, as an possibility, without delay jump into a few thing route of motion they decide on, on the identical time as minimizing any functionality threat and denying their functionality danger.

Chapter 7: The Epicure

This individual type, the Epicure, is not any doubt the most amusing and enthusiastic of all of the Enneagram. The Epicure is enthusiastic about almost each hobby and enjoy that they deem thrilling. They are the those who stay life with the form of mind-set that makes them seem like youngsters in a sweet keep as though the arena is theirs for the taking. They have a tendency to be curious, high-quality and function a keen feel of journey. Their gaze on the arena is one in every of substantial-open eyes as they live in a consistent country of excited anticipation for all of the extraordinary memories they expect to have. They are the sort that is bold and energetic, the kind maximum possibly to pursue their existence dreams, and to acquire this with a sense of humor that often coats a steelier sense of dedication.

Like the Loyal Skeptic, the Epicure is part of the Head Center, irrespective of the fact that that is not straight away apparent. The Epicure, for all their love of satisfaction, is likewise normally very arms on, pragmatic and likes to maintain loads of irons inside the fireplace usually. For example, your colleague who excels at multitasking may also well be an Epicure. The Epicure thinks in an anticipatory style, that's what makes them a part of the Head Center. They are typically thinking in advance, searching for to foresee what might appear. They like to anticipate on their toes and launch themselves into sports activities sports that cause them to think. The end result of that is that they will be then engaged in considering even greater subjects and doing responsibilities to the issue that they will finally get frazzled or distracted (regardless of the reality that this threshold is a lot better than it might be in the different types). But do no longer be misled, the Epicure isn't commonly a bookworm or perhaps an intellectual with the resource of any conventional perception, despite the fact that they is probably widely take a look at and honestly verbal—and may be of above common intelligence. Because their minds leap around from one idea to the following, the Epicure is exquisite at brainstorming sports activities activities or perhaps reading facts, making them very favored in an workplace setting. The Epicure is so authentic at doing this form of artwork because of the fact for them, it is interesting to experience the frenzy of mind. The delight of spontaneity itself frequently fuels their functionality to paintings for hours on prevent—as it does no longer feel to them like mere drudgery. For this identical cause, the Epicure loves to create huge overviews of a given difficulty depend in vicinity of taking area deep into the weeds. The Epicure is likewise much more likely to excel on the start of a creative method, in place of being a "closer."

Some of the inner workings of the Epicure consists of folks that see themselves as a "listing character," so you can hold their mind targeted on transferring in advance instead of spinning in place—which surely works to take away their hard-earned entertainment of an hobby. Other excessive first-rate features of the Epicure are that they regularly have flexible minds, and that they tend to be very short rookies. On the best hand, they're capable of absorb records—be it languages, techniques or statistics. On the alternative hand, they'll be also succesful to accumulate new manual skills, for example, they will have brilliant thoughts-body coordination, and high-quality motor competencies that make them pinnacle typists, musical virtuosos, tennis specialists or excessive-level repair women and men. The Epicure, way to those two sorts of competencies, can regularly be perceived because the quality "Renaissance man or woman."

As with all of the man or woman sorts, those competencies frequently encompass a disadvantage particularly at the same time as the Epicure we should their mind get out of stability. The Epicures' reputedly countless experience of interest and capacity to pick out up new capabilities quicker than others is also a deliver of problem for them. Because of this uncannily flair for obtaining such a lot of specific skills without an excessive amount of of a war, the Epicure can be out of vicinity approximately what unique direction to pursue. This can suggest they've got a dispersive life, with what looks like many dead ends, as they are attempting out a number of specific hats in their lives. The unique terrible thing of the prevailing of being proper at many stuff is that furthermore they do now not have a propensity to apprehend what they might do as they could have in the event that they needed to paintings tirelessly for years if you want to achieve them. Luckily, the Epicure in stability is capable of harness those massive offers. They show off personalities which is probably curious and agile, and therefore, their capability for obtaining new competencies lets in them to collect extremely good heights.

The root of the problem of the Epicure is the identical one that is shared by means of manner of all of the different forms of the Head Center. They do no longer understand a way to get into contact with their inner guidance assist tool. As with the Observer and the Loyal Skeptic, this lack of connectedness motives a terrible sense of inadequacy and worry in the Epicure. They have the high-quality of intentions, but they experience powerless to choose out a direction of motion a good way to be in keeping with those intentions; and in no way are they egocentric. They are as likely to conflict searching for what to do for themselves and for particular human beings. The Epicure tries to cope with this worry in special strategies. Their first line of defense is that they are looking to maintain themselves as occupied as viable, all of the time, to the element that they may growth insomnia. The Epicure thinks that as long as they may achieve success in know-how a manner to maintain their mind busy, they might preserve their fears at bay. This often consists of jumping into tasks for the destiny, it's their favored way to prevent bad feelings from without a doubt bursting into their aware awareness. In hundreds the same way, the Epicure is the form of person kind that has to keep on shifting; many those who choose out a nomadic lifestyle are Epicures who have misplaced their revel in of grounding. Activity and mobility work to stimulate their notion techniques, which excites them similarly until they spiral right into a veritable churning of idea and movement. That stated, they do now not toil uselessly; on the alternative, for all their affiliation with delight, the Epicure receives the hobby finished manner to their sensible nature.

Second, it is crucial to understand that the Epicure offers with this detachment from their internal steering guide machine with a way that can best be defined as trial and mistakes. Since they do not understand what is great, they genuinely attempt the whole lot and notice what sticks. The Epicure has a deep worry that they may in no way be capable of discover their actual purpose in lifestyles, their personal project assertion as it were, so they'll pass from element to element with hopes that some issue sticks. This constant looking can cause dilettantism and a stunting of the Epicure's proper exquisite functionality. When it goes on for too prolonged, the looking itself can emerge as an goal in and of itself, in place of a technique to an surrender. Their right judgment is that in the occasion that they can not have the factor in existence that truly makes them happy, why no longer enjoy themselves and function some of testimonies alongside the way as a compensation for this unhappy preference.

The method of trial and mistakes is on display even in mundane, each day sports. If you offer the Epicure a bowl of Halloween candy, you may see them hesitate in advance than deciding on, and they'll probably change their thoughts more than one instances (or extra, counting on how cushty they feel with you), and however enjoy regret about all the types of candy they did no longer get to attempt. As they hesitate, they'll be wondering, "what piece of candy do I actually need? What's the proper choice?" This is a totally excessive manner to relate to a few component as minor as selecting a candy address. If you ever plan a holiday with an Epicure, you can revel in a similar phenomenon. What is the amazing way to spend loose time? Where need to they pass? What want to they see after they get there? These questions cope with a existence in their very very own, and in an horrific Epicure, it can bring about missing out on a laugh. (Imagine consuming a Hershey's bar on the identical time as wishing you were eating a Reese's or touring Paris even as you dreamed of being in Rome).

With the whole thing said to date, you can probably wager that the Epicure will address situations with multiple options via way of seeking to do all of it – at the chance of diminishing the entirety within the method. In the rush to discover the maximum thrilling hobby or the most delicious meals, they'll be capable of bury their proper desire so deep down interior them that they end up no longer understanding what they in reality need.

The actual risk for an Epicure is the tendency to hurry into something it's miles they suppose they want and it pushes them to make terrible alternatives. Then they get caught in a awful spiral, wherein they experience a great deal much less and much less glad with the myriad topics they've got. They come to be detached from the present, stuck in their head, and then they enjoy those prolonged-favored activities through a veritable blur created through the fast firing in their minds. You can recognize this bring about an Epicure, due to the fact they'll seem uncharacteristically involved and pissed off, even to the issue of springing into anger, when they may be in a scenario that have to be interesting (like mountaineering up to the pinnacle of the Eiffel Tower for the primary time). As a surrender end result of their horrible alternatives, they'll similarly spiral down due to the fact they will have wasted valuable property, whether or not bodily, emotionally, or perhaps financially. The give up quit end result is that they might without problems wind up destroying their health, compromising their relationships, and depleting their rate kind of their in no way-finishing quest for happiness.

The Epicures are very optimistic person sorts. They are lively, dynamic and amusing to be round. They can without problem become the existence of the party, and for them, normal lifestyles can be a a laugh—at the identical time as they are in stability. They need to stay their lives to the fullest, in its smallest element. The Epicure is usually pleased with a heat humorousness. They are not the sort that risks taking themselves too significantly. Because the Epicure desires to sense fulfilled, satisfied and satisfied. When they manage to find out harmony inner themselves, their satisfaction and ardour for residing improves life for all the humans round them. The wholesome Epicure is able to remind absolutely all and sundry approximately the essential pleasures of gift.

The related styles of the Epicure are:

Wing: Loyal Skeptic 6

Wing: Protector 8

Security Type: Observer 5

Stress Type: Perfectionist 1

The most common, non-related appearance-alike sorts of the Epicure are:

Giver 2

Performer 3

Mediator 9

The opportunity of sorts (differing types to preserve in mind if Epicure is your top desire):

fifty two% Epicure 7

7% Giver 2

7% Observer 5

7% Loyal Skeptic 6

6% Mediator 9

5.Five% Perfectionist 1

Based on those possibilities, if you scored excessive at the Epicure check, there may be handiest a fifty % risk it is your accurate type, so keep with warning. There is also an 7% hazard of you being a Giver, an Observer or a Loyal Skeptic. There is a small, 6% danger that you are a Mediator, and a five.5% chance which you are a Perfectionist. This manner that you need to cautiously evaluation each different excessive ratings for your different assessments and then study the distinguishing sections under carefully to appearance if those want to in reality be your kind. Remember, if a positive type has a strong wing of 1 or the alternative, that can drastically have an impact on how the individual manifests itself. If you can't receive the sort you are, your emotions can be legitimate, or can be a give up end result of the horrific stereotypes you've got got heard about the sort, so make certain to find out any robust reactions you may have.

Myths About the Epicure

The Epicure is related to the sin of gluttony. They are omitted as superficial parents which might be best inquisitive about their non-public enjoyment. They are feared as now not being able to forming deep attachments with others or upholding commitments because of the reality they may be so frequently on the flow into. Epicures frequently are brushed off as willpower phobic.

Adjectives Describing the Epicure

On the extremely good thing, fun, short, charming, curious, concerned, engaged, spontaneous, amusing and cutting-edge. On the poor side, possessive, manic, unfavorable, burdened, rebellious, distracted, impulsive and narcissistic.

The Underlying Truths of the Epicure

The primary principle the Epicure has forgotten: Life gives each one humans a entire spectrum of opportunities that everybody is loose to revel in.

The Epicure wrongly believes: The international works to restrict and restrict humans, and via the ones obstacles takes away satisfaction.

The Epicure created these behaviors to: Avoid limitations by way of using manner of having as lots a laugh as viable whether or not or not this indicates over indulging in mind, evaluations, food and drink, sexual family participants or shopping.

The Characteristics that Define the Epicure

Because of these adaptive behaviors, the Epicure focuses their mind on: Obtaining as masses satisfaction as feasible in whatever area is maximum critical to them. They need to find interconnections amongst one-of-a-type geographical areas of information. They moreover like to spend time looking after themselves and gratifying their very very personal insatiable goals.

They placed their strength into: Having the maximum amusing viable. Staying excellent and dynamic. Being fascinating and nonthreatening. Always having the higher hand.

The Epicure desperately tries to keep away from: Limits, barriers, policies, boredom, being trapped, struggling, unhappiness and war of words.

The Epicure has those strengths: Finding the great in every situation irrespective of how tough. Making everything fun for others. Keeping a powerful outlook. Being useful. Creating revolutionary conditions. Having a detailed imaginative and prescient of the area. Sharing and spreading enthusiasm, even for simple, regular pleasures.

The Epicure communicates in the following way: Speeding thru lifestyles, leaping from scenario remember to undertaking depend, leaning on excuses even as challenged and they're open to endless opportunities.

The Sources of Stress, Anger and Defensiveness

The Epicure is careworn through manner of: Becoming overworked at the same time as it comes time to meet all the duties they have got dipped their toes into. Constantly making the identical mistakes because of the unwavering desire to keep away from ache. Being trapped by means of the use of the use of commitments. Trying to address being overworked.

The Epicure is angered approximately: Limitations, specially the ones placed on pleasure. Other people who do not percentage the equal fantastic life outlook.

The Epicure is defensive in the direction of: Anyone who attempts to spread a pessimistic mind-set.

Their anger and defensiveness are characterized as such: Efficient and direct, and as a consequence, short lasting. They can also located distinct people down with impulsive, hurtful insults, after which right away recover from it and circulate on – and now not understand their lingering resentment.

Personal Growth

Their final purpose is: To be determined in existence and to truly enjoy the hobby, man or woman or factor that is inside the the front of them inside the interim.

They can further this growth thru: Understanding how the superficial can block them from real amusement and the way looking for pride can be an avoidance of pain, appreciating other human beings's emotions, training self-compassion and expertise the regulations of an existence based entirely on satisfaction.

Their largest impediment is: Refusing to make one cause at a time, focusing too obsessively on themselves, being too outcomes distracted and insisting on having a superb temper even when it's far counterproductive.

Others can assist this increase via the use of: Questioning them at the same time as they may be attempting to disarm barriers through their enchantment, encouraging them to decide to 1 single opportunity, citing whilst they are trying to provide highbrow escapes thru planning multiple tasks (in location of committing to 1), assisting them after they choose to gradual down, even a bit bit and inspiring simplicity.

Practical Suggestions for the Epicure:

• Prioritize your fitness thru using primary food regimen and workout ideas.

• Pay hobby to over eating or over spending in times of pressure.

• Try to prioritize emotions of gratitude rather than lack.

• Acknowledge your emotions through meditation, remembering that they will be temporary.

•Remember to invite unique people how they experience.

•Consider the possibility of being an entrepreneur or self-hired in case you are suffering as an employee.

•Commit to finishing a assignment earlier than starting any other.

•Try to tell tales through sticking to the truth and the records without embellishment.

Famous Epicures in History

Steve Allen, Tim Allen, Desi Arnaz, Fred Astaire, Antonio Banderas, Jack Benny, Silvio Berlusconi, Leonard Bernstein, Chuck Berry, Jacqueline Bisset, Sonny Bono, Elayne Boosler, Terry Bradshaw, Kenneth Branagh, Richard Branson, Michael Caine, Joseph Campbell, Jim Carrey, Jackie Chan, Chevy Chase, Cher, George Clooney, Francis Ford Coppola, Katie Couric, Noel Coward, Tony Curtis, Hugh Downs, Michael Eisner, Douglas

Fairbanks Jr., Sarah Ferguson, Errol Flynn, Peter Fonda, Malcolm Forbes, George Foreman, Bob Fosse, Michael J. Fox, Benjamin Franklin, Galileo Galilei, Ava Gardner, John Gielgud, Cary Grant, George Hamilton, Tom Hanks, Richard Harris, Goldie Hawn, Marilu Henner, Ron Howard, Lauren Hutton, Mick Jagger, Thomas Jefferson, Steve Jobs, Magic Johnson, King Juan Carlos of Spain, Elton John, Michael Keaton, John F. Kennedy, Don King, Timothy Leary, Loretta Lynn, Ricky Martin, Meat Loaf, Dudley Moore, Eddie Murphy, Anthony Quinn, Ram Dass, Lee Remick, Geraldo Rivera, Ginger Rogers, Linda Ronstadt, David Lee Roth, Rosalind Russell, Babe Ruth, Martin Scorsese, Martin Short, Sissy Spacek, Britney Spears, Steven Spielberg, Robert Louis Stevenson, Barbra Streisand, Elizabeth Taylor, Lily Tomlin, Lana Turner, Ted Turner, Peter Ustinov, Dick Van Dyke, Vince Vaughn, Voltaire, Eli Wallach, Betty White, Robin Williams, Duke of Windsor, Jonathan

Winters, James Woods, William Wordsworth.

Related Types

Every persona type is inspired through the wings to the difficulty that they may mixture into in reality one in all them. If a personality type has a strong wing, it will make a massive effect on the person's character.

Loyal Skeptic 6 (wing): An Epicure with a strong 6 wing will be greater reliable and responsible but may additionally even be afflicted by greater tension.

Protector 8 (wing): An Epicure with a strong 8 wing may be greater aggressive but moreover amusing. They can also will be inclined to be materialistic.

Observer 5 (security kind): When the Epicure is capable of pass to the powerful aspect in their protection kind, they are in a position to show inwards. This is superb because of the truth they will be extra introspective and plenty less flashy. They can learn how to receive the extremes of life, brilliant and terrible. They also are extra important and, therefore, are taken extra extensively with the useful resource of those they appreciate. They learn how to get in touch with their fears, that could reason large self-discovery.

When the Epicure is pressured to move to the bad aspect of their protection type, they'll get pushy and unconcerned about what others assume. They turn inwards to the factor of self-absorption and shirking in their duties.

Perfectionist 1 (stress type): When the Epicure is capable of skip to the brilliant factor of their pressure type, they boom their productivity and are able to follow through in choice to flit from detail to trouble. They are also able to be extra practical of their choices and grow to be more worried with making other human beings satisfied.

When the Epicure is forced to transport to the horrible thing in their stress type, they lose all sense of humor approximately themselves. They hang to black and white wondering at their fee. They can be cynical, petty, judgmental and merciless. They may be higher approximately finishing responsibilities however show off obsessive inclinations that overshadow any gain.

Overlaps Between the Epicure and Other Non-associated Types

Giver 2: The Epicure is similar to the Giver due to their shared active attitudes. They are humans pleasers who may additionally also be seductive in their behaviors inside the course of others. They range due to the truth Epicures need to attention on themselves and what they want and might without problem become self-absorbed. The Giver, instead, is always targeted on distinctive human beings and clean to sacrifice his experience of self.

Performer 3: There are severa similarities some of the Performer and the Epicure because of the reality each are busy and energetic. They are optimists who need to get matters completed. They moreover prefer to avoid horrible emotions of any kind. The vital difference is that Epicures are focused on their very own pleasures to the element in which they may be defined as entitled or egocentric. They sincerely keep in mind they have got each right to maintain their alternatives open and may be envious if a person tells them otherwise. Performers, on the alternative, aren't driven via way of pleasure however with the useful resource of maintaining an first-rate picture. In order to get and maintain onto this outside, societal approval, they will sacrifice their very non-public inner feel of self. Performers also are extra concerned with performance than Epicures.

Romantic 4: These sorts are often considered look-alikes due to their similar depth, idealism and preference for adventure and stimulation. Both sorts are deeply dedicated to residing a existence via their acute emotional schools. The largest difference comes in terms in their mood. Epicures are energetic, high-quality and immoderate first-rate. They are trying to find pride and keep away from pain. Romantics are the alternative as they will be characterised through melancholic feelings.

Mediator nine: One of the valuable shared traits some of the Mediator and the Epicure is that each would love to have a exquisite, happy life. In order to gain it, they may be possibly to be smooth to get along with and battle adverse.

Chapter 8: The Protector

One of the primary attributes of the Protector, character type 8, is the truth that they honestly experience undertaking hard themselves—and love to offer one of a kind human beings exciting possibilities which is probably purported to venture them to enhance themselves in some way. For this cause, the Protector will regularly discover themselves within the feature of a teacher, a mentor or a educate. Furthermore, the Protector has an inclination to be greater charismatic than the opposite kinds. Their aim is to persuade others to comply with them into all sorts of activities, whether or not it's far as mundane as managing a own family, as grandiose as commencing a modern day business enterprise enterprise undertaking, or as earth shattering as waging warfare or making peace. Thus, many Protectors have a tendency to be CEOs and worldwide leaders. Luckily, the Protector normally is endowed with a combination of the bodily and intellectual abilities that they need to be most persuasive to others. For this purpose, greater often than not, they are able to get what they want for themselves and, if in stability, they regularly manipulate to benefit the very best stages of success in all areas in their lives that they take a look at themselves.

One of the maximum obvious dispositions a good way to let you spot the Protector from a distance is their exceptional revel in of self-control and their boundless strength. These functions, which often require a brilliant deal of effort in distinctive types, are in fact what fuels the Protector and purpose them to sense alive within the global. The Protector is satisfied to use their boundless strength to make adjustments round them. They are the kind of oldsters which are hungry to make their mark, but in addition they need to make adjustments to help guard others from ache (as a stop end result, the call of the individual kind). Since they examine from an early age that in an effort to be powerful Protectors, they'll should be sturdy, willful and continual. They work to increase their non-public persistence in themselves and searching for out others who percent the ones tendencies.

One of the topics that the Protector hates maximum is at the same time as others try to manage them, or actually have strength over them. They are fiercely unbiased, whether or not it's far in phrases in their intellectual and sexual nicely-being, or their social and economic fitness. They will exert a large quantity in their boundless power to make certain that they may be capable of keep and growth some thing power they may have, and to attain this for so long as humanly possible. It does not keep in mind what profession path or social popularity the Protector may also moreover have whether or not or now not they're a house painter or a developer, a freelancer or a business organization titan, the pinnacle of a family or a spiritual network leader. The Protector flourishes with the useful resource of being in charge in their realm, but massive or small. Their desire to leave a mark—and now not to be forgotten—is a feature of the Protector.

In their choice to make a large effect, the Protector is satisfied to carry out duties by myself, quite a number different type. They is probably described as proper "rugged individualists." Amongst all the kinds of the Enneagram, they're those who most need to be unbiased humans; they actively face up to feeling like they very non-public some thing, no matter how small. The Protector is the sort of person who, inside the unusual occurrence that they may reluctantly take shipping of a tiny "mortgage," will then go out of their manner to go lower back the amount of money borrowed as speedy as possible, in advance than any cut-off date is near. The Protector is the most effective who will continuously refuse to fall apart to social stress. They are satisfied to fly in the face of horrific feelings, whether or not or not its humiliation or tension, and could disregard any viable consequences of their moves. True, the Protector is frequently cognizant of the reviews of various human beings, but they'll be the kind this is least in all likelihood to be encouraged thru those reviews. The Protector is happy to go approximately their corporation, minding their very personal goals with such energy of mind that they inspire in a few, and located worry in others.

It might in all likelihood seem contradictory, but the Protector does dread being physical harmed; but, their best most essential worry is being controlled or losing their power. Thus, the Protector has a bent to be quite tough, and makes a brilliant athlete or soldier as they're able to take a whole lot of bodily pressure without complaining. This is mostly a right element, but it could backfire as they're regularly blind to how tough they really are. By taking their health as a right, they will no longer do the regular matters which may be required to keep it like having a healthy warmth up and funky down routine for workout, getting sufficient sleep and keeping a balanced weight loss plan. When they're in relationships, they'll furthermore be oblivious to the health issues of these round them due to the fact that they have a dishonest to be so properly endowed of their non-public physicality. Another problem with this excellent bodily energy is that they use it as a shape of protection. By being imperturbable, they will be looking to guard their fragile emotional nation and keep others at a amazing emotional distance within the interest of preserving themselves. This, of course, results in feelings of isolation that can be difficult to conquer thinking about the truth that they now not regularly reveal this to every body, even the ones internal their most intimate circle. However, they without a doubt do have a gentle center of vulnerability on the coronary heart of all that durability; it certainly takes a tremendous deal of staying strength to have them open up and reveal it.

One of the strategies that the Protector builds this armor is through preserving themselves busy – and no longer doing meaningless matters, doing subjects that allows you to appreciably enhance their worldwide for themselves and others. The fee of all this, however, is that they danger losing emotional contact with most of the most crucial people of their lives. People who're near them will often locate themselves complaining the longer they spend together, and the Protector's emotional armor will become extra painful to put on. The Protector has trouble information court cases as they feel as no matter the reality that all the paintings they do for absolutely everyone spherical them ought to greater than capture up at the emotional distance.

In reality, at the same time because the Protector gets confronted via individuals who choice more emotional intimacy from them, they become feeling misunderstood. These confrontations will be inclined to backfire and result in the Protector in addition distancing themselves from their loved ones in response. This is because their formidable look and funky demeanor is essentially a mask for his or her everyday emotions of ache and rejection. They rarely talk about this, however, due to the reality the Protector refuses to admit any shape of vulnerability to in reality everybody, even to themselves. They experience this is tantamount to freely giving their electricity. Because they worry approximately being rejected in some manner, the Protector likes to make a pre-emptive strike. If they fear their partner desires to divorce them, they will request a divorce first. If they'll be in jeopardy of losing their jobs, they'll stop first. Even if they're being humiliated or criticized, they might lash out in the direction of the individual in advance than they get a hazard to assault. Not especially, the Protector has a bent to go through of their relationships with others. For the Protector, loving someone manner to provide away their strength, and that is the hardest emotion of interested in them to enjoy.

The stronger the Protector protects themselves emotionally, the weaker they come to be. They are an increasing number of touchy even as someone questions their authority and notice it as a likely attempt to undermine them. They truely can close themselves down as a way to protect themselves, genuinely so they're clearly inaccessible to everybody.

Fortunately, an emotionally wholesome Protector is resourceful and pragmatic. They are constructive approximately accomplishing a few element project and overcoming boundaries. Their steady inner pressure allows them to persevere thru an prolonged, tough trial. The Protector is the proper in shape for an extended-distance courting as they will consistent themselves and look ahead to their accomplice to come back once more home, and do not be afflicted by way of using the regular lack of bodily proximity. The Protector is glad to take an initiative and make topics appear for themselves and others. They live with passion however additionally restraint, so they'll be frequently respected as honorable. They aren't likely to abuse their authority, despite the truth that they continuously appearance to consolidate it, and that they make herbal leaders who very own a strong, confident presence. Their connection to fact gives them massive commonplace experience. They are not afraid to make alternatives, nor are they worried approximately sitting within the heat seat while their choice necessarily runs afoul of a person. They will typically generally tend to take care of the pursuits of the powers that be (which means that the Protector might be "agency guy"), but further they have a propensity to be fair and avoids playing favorites. The Protector works to use their abilties and energy to make a better worldwide for all of the human beings they've got in their lives.

The related kinds of the Protector are:

Wing: Epicure 7

Wing: Mediator 9

Security Type: Giver 2

Stress Type: Observer 5

The most common non-related look-alike sorts of the Protector are:

Perfectionist 1

Romantic 4

Loyal Skeptic 6

The chance of kinds (different sorts to take into account if Protector is your pinnacle choice):

37% Protector

sixteen.Five% Loyal Skeptic,

sixteen% Perfectionist

eight% Romantic

7% Epicure

6% Mediator

Based on those chances, in case you scored immoderate on the Protector take a look at, there's absolutely exceptional a 37% risk it's miles your accurate type, so please be conscious earlier than forming conclusions. In truth, there may be additionally a 16.Five% risk of your being a Loyal Skeptic, a 16% threat of being a Perfectionist an 8% danger of being a Romantic, a 7% chance of being an Epicure and a 6% hazard of being a Mediator. If you scored excessive on those exams as well, study the distinguishing sections under cautiously to appearance if those ought to surely be your type. Remember, if a positive type has a sturdy wing of one or the opposite, which can notably have an effect on how the character manifests itself. If you cannot take delivery of the kind you're, your feelings can be legitimate, or may be a give up end result of the terrible stereotypes you have got have been given heard approximately the sort, so make sure to discover any strong reactions you can have.

The Myths of the Protector

The horrific stereotypes of the Protector are toughness and being competitive. This is the most masculine of the man or woman sorts, due to this that woman eights regularly revel in social problems. Eights can be all or now not some issue, simply so can be exhilarating or threatening for the ones round them.

The Adjectives Describing the Protector

On the terrific aspect, they may be direct, assertive, dependable, energetic, all of the manner all the way down to earth and protecting. On the horrible side, they will be skeptical, aggressive, impulsive, commanding, blunt, and rebellious.

The Underlying Truths of the Protector

The number one principle the Protector has forgotten: Everyone has identical get proper of entry to to truth and innocence.

The Protector wrongly believes: The worldwide is unfair, so hunt or be hunted.

The Protector created those behaviors to compensate: Imposing their beliefs on different people, hiding their weak spot to benefit a sense of inner value, developing insatiable energy and a eager intuition.

The Characteristics that Define the Protector

Because of those adaptive behaviors: The protector makes a speciality of obtaining electricity, retaining manipulate, policing justice and leaping into movement proper away.

They positioned their energy into: Controlling everything feasible and annoying recognize.

They desperately attempt to keep away from: Any signal of weakness or uncertainty and relying on other humans.

They have the ones strengths: Being courageous, sincere, decisive and honest. Maintaining intensity to the element of energizing others. Clearly accepting management roles.

They communicate in the following manner: They are direct and are considered authoritarians. They are open about their preference for control.

The Sources of Stress, Anger and Defensiveness

They are forced with the resource of: Any chance to their authority. Being now not able to restore any perceived unfairness. Being compelled to be more self-contained. Acknowledging physical obstacles.

They are angered about: Injustice. Feeling tricked. Weak people.

They are defensive inside the path of: People who don't observe orders. People who try to manipulate them.

Their anger and defensiveness are characterised as such: Through overt, expressive anger and battle of phrases. Seeking revenge.

Personal Growth

Their final aim is: To understand the basics of human decency.

They can further this growth via manner of: Allowing others to provoke moves, getting to know to channel anger in preference to suppress or specific it and writing down insights to keep away from forgetting or being in denial. Observing whilst their intensity inspires and even because it negatively influences remarkable humans. Practicing patience. Counting to ten earlier than talking. Waiting a few hours or days earlier than taking movement. Striving for a win-win final effects.

Their largest obstacle is: Lack of personal attention about controlling behaviors. Refusing to renowned weaknesses. Believing that energy have to be maintained at all fees.

Others can assist this increase with the useful resource of: Encouraging compromise, assisting Protectors once they open up, ensuring to speak their reality to the Protector and stand their floor against them.

Practical Suggestions for the Protector:

•Take a path in negotiation.

•Investigate the belongings of your anger in treatment.

•Take time to understand cherished ones verbally

•Write down your expectations for your self and share with a trusted friend to find out the realistic ones.

•Take day trip of each day for a modern undertaking.

•Play a game with the purpose of getting a laugh.

www.ingramcontent.com/pod-product-compliance
Lightning Source LLC
Chambersburg PA
CBHW062139020426
42335CB00013B/1272